Green Wisdom

A Guide for Anyone to Start, Engage and Energize a Sustainability Team

Nikki Pava

Copyrighted © 2019 by Nikki Pava
All rights reserved

No part of this publication may be reproduced, in whole or in part, in any form or by any means, without the prior written consent of the author or as expressly permitted by law.

Please purchase only authorized electronic editions and do not participate in or encourage electronic piracy of copyrighted materials.

ORDERING INFORMATION
Quantity sales: Special discounts are available on quantity purchases by corporations and schools (for course adoption use). For details, please email: thanks@alegriapartners.com.

ISBN: 9781091582088

~Thank You~

To my little family
Aaron
Jaidyn
Astrid

For sharing your Green Wisdom
with me every day.

I am forever grateful.

My gratitude goes out to the leaders at the following companies for sharing their Green Wisdom, and for the teams full of passionate people who are shaping our future.

TABLE OF CONTENTS

FOREWORD by Christiana Figueres 7

INTRODUCTION 11

Chapter One: Building Your Sustainability Team 19
    Sustainability Teams and B Corporation – A Combination for Success 39

Chapter Two: The First Steps To Create Your Sustainability Team 47
    Salesforce: Providing Vision and Leadership to Teams of all Levels 63

Chapter Three: Getting Your Executives Engaged 69
    Dumpster Diving Creates the Connection 83

Chapter Four: Make Your Approach Unique 87
    A Different Approach to Sustainability Efforts 105

Chapter Five: From Breakdowns to Breakthroughs 109
    Re-inspiring the Team 127

Chapter Six: Connecting To The Community 129
    Community Engagement Menu 139

Chapter Seven: Benefits of Participation 145
    The Earthforce Ohana Group 159

Chapter Eight: Your Fun Campaigns Can Bring Results 161
    The Big Picture: A Year-Long Sustainability Road Map Everyone Can Use 177

Chapter Nine: Inspiring Your Company to "Walk the Talk" 183
    A Cross-Departmental Team in Practice 197

Chapter Ten: Shaping Your Company Culture 201
    Gratitude Puts Everything into Perspective 211

Chapter Eleven: The Power of Proof 215
    Comprehensive Resources 217
    Convergent Resources 227
    Corporate Commitment 233

FOREWORD

When nations, industries, business leaders and communities began to understand that designing a sustainable future is an economic opportunity - not an economic burden - a pivotal turning point occurred in the global conversation surrounding climate change.

Innovators and influencers realized that building a future that contains clean air and better health, intelligent transportation, livable cities, and energy security will stimulate growth and improve bottom lines. With that understanding—the understanding that sustainability is about constraining the negative (e.g. greenhouse gases) in order to precipitate the positive (e.g. human flourishing) —comes optimism.

In the face of global challenges, optimism is the deliberate choice of living and working out of the deep conviction that humans can come together, in any size and setting, from many different backgrounds, to build a hopeful future. When you examine the bigger picture, it only makes sense that if so many of our problems were caused by our penchant for independence and self-focus, those problems must be addressed with intentional interdependence. Interdependence is the model of health we see at work in the natural world, and for our own sake, it is a model we must replicate.

Every day new investors and stakeholders are recognizing the very real risks that are inherent in the old, carbon-based economy. They have begun to understand that environmental integrity is not a feel-good, second-tier solution; is the prime key to efficiency and profit. Implementing this efficiency through circular designs, by eliminating waste and utilizing cleaner forms of energy is not only good for our environment – but more than that it is good for business.

There is a long journey ahead and we don't know all the steps that will lead us to our destination.

However, our destination is clear: a decarbonized, highly resilient and collaborative economy. This destination is universally beneficial. It is in the best interest of all people. We will move towards it on different paths, guided by our unique contexts and communities, but in every case, the ability to clearly visualize and articulate our goal is the key to moving forward and requires our best and highest efforts.

The corporate Sustainability Teams featured in this book are giving vision to this future, even as they make it our reality. They are ignoring political noise and distractions, choosing to instead exercise the stubborn optimism that is required to disassemble problems and manufacture solutions from the pieces. Fueled by the creativity of diversity, these groups are changing the role of business in an uncertain future. They are doing this because they know it is in the best interest of their business, their stakeholders, and their customers, at the same time as it is in the best interest of our planet. The benefit imperatives stack up and reinforce each other.

Competition has long been a driving force in human innovation. It will, and should, continue to be so. But in the business of the new economy—a work of profitable restoration—I have found that there is an even more powerful force than rivalry and confrontation: radical collaboration.

We know that the whole is often far greater than the sum of its parts, and in the work of a Sustainability Team (be it a gathering of line workers or entire nations), we see this truth take shape quite tangibly. Behaviors are changed, small actions are multiplied, and ripples become tide-turning waves.

As you learn from these inspiring Sustainability Teams and orchestrate your own, know that collaboration and interdependence are the cornerstones of a real, lasting economy. Take every opportunity to inject transformational optimism into your conversations, and allow the power of interdependence to change the way you think, act, and create.

You will build a future you are proud to pass on to the next generation, but you will not do so alone.

Embrace the freedom of this interconnectedness and then go get to work.

We're counting on you.

— **_Christiana Figueres_**
*Executive Secretary of the UN Framework Convention on Climate Change (2010-2016)
Founding Partner, Global Optimism*

INTRODUCTION

My sustainability journey began 5,000 miles from home. While working for the Japan Times, I had the unique opportunity to live in major business hubs across the globe—Berlin, Bangkok, Dubai—and interview the CEOs and managing directors of some of the biggest companies in the world—Sony, Toyota, Schneider Logistics, Bayer AG, and more.

I conducted hundreds of interviews with major business leaders. In each, I asked about their companies' business model, their customers, and the next new exciting product they were launching. I also always asked about their companies' social and environmental initiatives. "I see that you're developing a hotel for thousands of people right on the edge of the beautiful Persian Gulf," I opened, "do you have a plan in place to protect the sea life and the nearby beaches?" Or, "Where will all the people who live in the tiny homes in that community relocate when construction begins on your multi-million-dollar real estate development?"

More often than not, my interviewee's face would turn blank and a rapid shift in conversation topic was sure to follow.

While there were many differences between the companies I interviewed, I began to notice an unfortunate common thread: almost none of these industry leaders had made climate change awareness a legitimate factor of their business model or developed a "green" strategy for the future. At this point, around the start of the new millennium, not one of these companies had a Sustainability Team in place or any way for employees to combine their personal passions with their careers.

Knowing the monumental influence of business on people, cultures, and societies, I realized that the world was in need of a global transformation of "business as usual." If large and small companies alike made small shifts toward sustainability, the impact would be enormous. I also realized that the tools needed to accomplish this transformation were not tools at all—they were people. The individuals that made up these businesses already had the power and resources to develop programs to positively contribute to their community and environment. They just needed to be empowered and unleashed.

That realization led me back to California, where I began working with businesses to start, engage, and energize Sustainability Teams.

Times Have Changed

In 2016, the United Nations Global Compact and Accenture Strategy conducted the largest-ever CEO sustainability study, gathering information from over 1,000 CEOs from more than 100 countries. Their results found that 97% of the chief executive officers "believe that sustainability is important to the future success of their business,"[1] 49% "believe that business will be the single most important factor in delivering the United Nations Sustainable Development Goals."[2]

This is a tremendous change from when I was conducting interviews nearly twenty years ago! The link between the economy and the environment is now well documented. Unfortunately, awareness doesn't always translate to behavior, and it will be our actions, not our intentions, that shape the environment of our future.

So what happens when these good intentions are actually put to the test? Despite almost universal awareness of the need for sustainability in business, a 2016 Bain & Company survey found shockingly low levels of goal achievement. Upon surveying 301 companies engaged in sustainability transformations, the management consulting firm found that only 2% actually met or exceeded their sustainability goals. 81% reported diluted results, and 16% failed to achieve even half of their original projections.[3]

Part of this gap can be explained by the fact that many groups working on corporate sustainability issues have been unofficially organized, meeting only intermittently as volunteer schedules allow. These teams have often lacked the clear vision and knowledge needed to set measurable reduction goals.

Though they may have been endorsed by the company, their efforts were more for show than to effectively achieve long-term results effectively, and they have had little or no influence on the company's core mission.

Thankfully, these groups are also in a state of tremendous evolution. Known by many names—Environmental Stewardship Committees, Sustainability Councils, or the standard Green Team—Sustainability Teams have created a new role for themselves in company business models. They are no longer special interest groups. They are becoming solution switchboards, engaging every department in the business to execute social and sustainable initiatives that impact all types of stakeholders. By educating and equipping current team members to tackle the seemingly disconnected sustainability issues that face their departments, they empower all levels of a workforce, helping enhance and retain top talent.

Dumpster dive by dumpster dive, Sustainability Teams are turning expensive waste removal practices into upcycling programs that generate profit. They are providing leadership to their company's ISO 14001 strategy, B Corp application process, and Global Reporting Initiative programs, building valuable brand awareness and tapping new corners of the market.

As you'll see, these teams are making more than soap, computer servers, and non-stop flights. They are taking apart problems and manufacturing sustainability from the pieces.

It Starts With You
As an owner, you strive to cut costs without compromising your commitments to quality and integrity. As an employee, you wonder how to bridge the gap between your highest ideals and the realities of the ecological impact of your work. Maybe you have a seed of an idea for a sustainable future, but how do you nurture that idea, allowing it to grow into a thoughtful and thriving sustainability program that makes a positive impact on the planet? What can you do to inspire and lead a team that designs regenerative strategies and systemic solutions, while also having a lot of fun?

Or perhaps you already serve on a Sustainability Team, but you struggle to find the tools and resources you need to gain momentum and reach meaningful milestones. You and your team need role models to inspire and guide you towards reaching your full potential.

The following chapters explore how more than ten companies have leveraged the work of their Sustainability Team and integrated the group's initiatives into their operations. Sustainability Team leaders share their Green Wisdom—how their teams originated, how they embed their work into the corporate business model, and the best practices they use to promote team unity, re-inspire members when momentum decreases, and implement fun and unique programs.

The best news is – these Sustainability Teams aren't made of external consultants or Silicon Valley fixers. As a result of contributions from warehouse workers and flight attendants, CEOs and salespeople, the innovative businesses featured in this book have:

- set (and achieved!) public-facing sustainability goals
- invigorated employees
- engaged and retained top talent
- cut costs
- increased profits
- decreased waste and energy output
- built connections with local communities

In each of these companies, high-functioning Sustainability Teams are using engaging campaigns with multiple entry points to create a "climate-conscious" culture that promotes health for employees, executives, shareholders, and the environment.

Growing Your Seeds
Green Wisdom is a collection of examples, frameworks, and tools that the best Sustainability Team leaders in the field have learned along the way. Take these stories and use them as a source of inspiration for your programs and initiatives.

Of course, every company is different. Initiatives and programs that work perfectly for one company may not work at all for another—even in the same industry. Customize the overall ideas to suit your company culture and business model, and you and your team will produce results worthy of a sequel to this book!

My hope is that *Green Wisdom: A Guide for Anyone to Start, Engage and Energize a Sustainability Team* inspires sustainability leaders like you to do good, to create valuable and engaging initiatives for employees, and to develop strategies that will show that your company's level of commitment to its social and environmental values is as important as making a profit.

1

Building Your Sustainability Team

It Started as an Idea
There is no fixed formula to make a Sustainability Team come to fruition. Each blossoms and grows differently. The companies interviewed for this book all have different stories to share about their team's inception. Some green initiatives started from nothing more than the vision of an enthusiastic team member, while other teams organically unfolded out of an earth-based event that inspired executives to transform their corporate structure.

Through conversations and interviews with highly successful teams, I've found that Sustainability Teams generally emerge as a result of a simple idea, or through the actions of a few specific people who have a sustainable vision for the company's future. An idea sparks action. These actions then begin to impact everyone on the team, others in the company, customers and clients, and even local communities.

Sustainability initiatives that work from the bottom-up are a great way to engage employees. The founders of these Sustainability Teams put effort into recruiting other team members and took the initiative to create and develop organically growing programs and campaigns that continue to bring awareness to their company's sustainability strengths and weaknesses. As these teams developed and gained momentum, businesses found that they were making valuable contributions to many different aspects of the company.

Before sharing the origin stories of some of these successful teams, let's first outline the general responsibilities and roles of a Sustainability Team.

What Does a Sustainability Team Do?
Your Sustainability Team's primary role is to work with executive teams to coordinate initiatives and ensure that they align with the company's needs and vision. For the most part, this translates into a few fairly specific activities:

Organize corporate campaigns and events related to sustainability:
- Water usage and contamination reduction

- Waste management – including recycling, composting, audits and paper reduction
- Energy Reduction – including bike-to-work, light usage, and green energy substitution
- Overall climate change awareness

Coordinate planet-themed events, usually integrated with sustainability campaigns, such as:
- Earth Day
- World Water Day
- Global Wind Day

Work with the Sustainability Department to ensure that all actions align with the company's overarching mission:
- Establish eco-friendly purchasing activities
- Reduce the consumption of products that adversely impact the environment
- Substitute eco-friendly products when possible for conventional products in use
- Develop guidelines for suppliers and vendors

Obtain certifications and endorsements that pertain to your company's industry:
- Join Green Business organizations
- Support the company in gaining Fair Trade International or B Corporation certification
- Join a trade organization such as the World Fair Trade Organization

Many Sustainability Teams also:
- Develop volunteer opportunities for team members to make a positive impact on the climate both inside and outside the company
- Create engaging and fun opportunities to share green wisdom with fellow employees to help them learn about sustainability
- Establish communication avenues between the company executives and stakeholders, in addition to structures to share sustainability information and events

Sustainability Teams are usually either volunteer, grassroots, or company-mandated initiatives that generate positive involvement on many levels. Volunteer teams begin with a small group of individuals who work to develop a keen understanding of their company's mission, strengths, and weaknesses related to sustainability. Mandated teams can arise as a result of city or government environmental regulations that a company must follow, or from an executive's desire to build a more sustainable company future.

Once the team is founded, one of the first steps you can take is recruiting additional team members and generating awareness. That awareness is leveraged into practical steps like reductions in waste, water, and energy usage, and changes in business habits. Pursuing sustainability certifications and endorsements helps to tell the story of your company's progress and can serve as a platform for continued community engagement through volunteer opportunities and education.

Grant Writing Success
The Environmental Stewardship Committee at Self-Help Credit Union and Ventures Fund (SHCU), like many other sustainability initiatives we will examine throughout this book, began as the result of a great idea. Its inception and early success were driven entirely by a group of employees that created a grassroots campaign to lead the transformation of SHCU into a triple-bottom-line organization. This committee started small, with easy-to-attain actions, yet the team and the campaigns grew over time, "snowballing" to educate teams across the organization and reaching out to new teams and new branches as the organization grew.

In the beginning, individuals at Self-Help came together to advocate for policy and operational changes and discover solutions for simple office challenges, such as finding ways to eliminate styrofoam in break rooms and creating processes to easily purchase more eco-friendly alternatives. The early founders dedicated a considerable amount of time to get other employees excited about sustainability and garner participation from a broader base to grow their grassroots campaigns.

One of the ways this volunteer group at Self-Help reached out to potential new members was by creating a campaign called "The Great Paper Smackdown." Employees on each floor of the SHCU office building competed with other floors to see who could use the least amount of paper during a given time. Team members loved competing with one another in this fun, free, and engaging campaign. With this simple contest, Self-Help's "Environmental

Stewardship Committee" (as they named themselves) set the tone for staff engagement.

Eventually, the initial group of volunteers realized that they needed support and leadership to continue these types of initiatives. They wanted to amplify their impact and take the organization's sustainability goals even deeper, yet everyone still needed to focus on their day jobs. A few motivated people on the committee parlayed their fundraising skills to secure a grant so the organization could hire a full-time Sustainability Director.

With funding secured to support a staff person for two years, Self-Help hired Melissa Malkin-Weber as the organization's first Green Initiatives Manager. While volunteers still drive the Environmental Stewardship Committee, Malkin-Weber is responsible for helping teams across the organization identify and implement opportunities to have a bigger environmental impact while achieving their team goals."

Greening the Blue Skies
Sustainability is a tricky problem for airlines. Very few people equate "being green" with flying on a 300-foot-long cylinder of metal that burns five gallons of fuel a mile. The success stories from Alaska Airlines and Horizon Air demonstrate that sustainability is possible, even in an industry that uses a large number of resources.

Alaska Airlines is the 5th largest carrier in the US and flies to Mexico, Canada and Costa Rica. Horizon is an award-winning regional airline operating in the Pacific Northwest and West Coast of the United States using a combination of turbo propeller planes and Embraer jets. Alaska Air Group owns both companies, making them "sister companies." Horizon's environmental story is similar to Self-Help Credit Union's; this award-winning green team started with a small group of passionate catering employees and flight attendants who worked together on an informal basis to make a massive shift in the overall business.

In the 80's, Horizon Air's flight attendants and catering staff realized that waste management was both a fundamental problem in the skies and something that they could help solve. In most cases, there were no recycling facilities at the airports and no guidelines or policies mandated by the airlines themselves. To remedy this situation, a few flight attendants and members of the catering staff would merely collect recyclable materials from flights, put them into their cars once they landed, and take them home or to a recycling facility in their free time. They disliked seeing used cups and cans going straight into the landfill once the planes landed.

A report published by the National Resource Defense Council (NRDC) in 2006 labeled the airline industry detrimental to the planet, pointing to airline waste as a significant cause.[2] The first line of the short article that introduced NRDC's yearlong study of the airline industry states, "The U.S. airline industry discards enough aluminum cans each year to build 58 Boeing 747 airplanes, along with thousands of tons of plastics, magazines, and newspapers."[3] While Horizon's efforts were still dependent on their grassroots initiative, the team took the NRDC article to heart. The staff involved in the guerilla recycling activities knew they were doing a good job, but their contributions were unmeasured, preventing them from building the concrete data needed to expand the initiatives. The volunteers (the generous flight attendants and catering staff members) went into overdrive, starting to measure their in-flight waste and recyclables - an essential step toward waste reduction.

Horizon Air found that it had a 67% diversion rate, meaning of the entire company's inflight waste, only one-third of it ended up in a landfill. To compare, no other airline had recycling initiatives at this time (about 2008), although some might have been collecting aluminum cans. While this was a significant achievement, the team at Horizon felt that there was still room for improvement. The volunteers banded together and focused their sights on a big dream, and in 2010 the grassroots team applied for and won the "Business Generator Recycler of the Year" award from the Washington State Recycling Association. Later, an article about airline recycling appeared in *Time Magazine* and shared that Horizon had reached a 67% diversion rate.[4] This milestone achievement helped to spark sustainability initiatives at Alaska Airlines.

Around the time of Horizon's first efforts into sustainability, Jacqueline Drumheller, who was in the Environmental Compliance department at Alaska, had a breakthrough. She had many ideas about decreasing waste on the airplanes and in corporate offices but had been unable to find an opportunity to communicate them to anyone at the airlines who could take action. One fateful day, she spotted the CEO of Alaska Airlines alone in the hallway waiting for an upcoming meeting with the Vice President.

Drumheller realized that she had a golden opportunity to share her green wisdom with the CEO, particularly about developing sustainability strategies at the company. At this point, she recalls, "the awareness was at an all-time high and I didn't think the company was doing enough." Drumheller wanted to make change happen at Alaska and she had her chance.

She introduced herself and shared her exciting ideas. Though she couldn't gauge his thoughts when he left for his meeting, in less than two hours she received a message from the VP saying that the CEO was interested in hearing more of her thoughts on the airline's sustainability initiatives.

At the same time, a small and informal Green Team at Alaska was starting. Drumheller shared with the small group that it was essential to quickly draft a proposal with a few well-thought-out ideas to the CEO while there was momentum. "When we first launched," Drumheller remembers, "the energy was so high and everyone wanted to do something. We drew people from all over the organization."

In 2008, the informal Alaska Airlines Green Team was rolled into one of the many affinity groups at the company. Drumheller also transitioned from environmental compliance to a new role as Sustainability Manager, making her responsible for the management and development of sustainability strategies and initiatives. She dedicated herself to ensuring that Alaska continued to be a leader in airline sustainability, and in her new role she was finally empowered to focus on in-flight waste and increasing energy efficiency. Jacqueline's efforts, combined with the informal "Green Team," helped develop a new corporate consciousness among employees. However, there was not enough widespread support for sustainability to make progress on the same scale as Horizon's recycling accomplishments.

In 2010, when the *Time* magazine article about Horizon was published, an executive at Alaska read the article and wondered why the airline wasn't putting more energy into waste and recycling management, while the much smaller Horizon Air was winning awards. This, in addition to launching a biofuels initiative with other aviation leaders, helped put the pieces into place. For the first time, executives saw sustainability as a business opportunity - both for saving money on items going to the landfill and for the recognition that the company could gain for their sustainability actions. In this way, the "win" in the sustainability landscape at Horizon helped to garner more financial and logistical support for Alaska's Green Team initiatives.

Members of Alaska's new Green Team created a proposal full of simple solutions to reduce resource use, such as strategies for in-flight recycling, recycling oil cans (each plane gets five quarts a day) and changing office printers from printing one-sided to double-sided. The blossoming Green Team also added the phrase "environmental stewardship" into the company's value statement, making sustainability a public-facing core value of the company (the company's mission statement has since changed).

Because of the efforts of the Green Team at sister company Alaska Airlines, a more formal in-flight recycling effort was created for both airlines, alleviating the recycling burden from flight-attendant volunteers. Now, all departments have their own waste and energy reduction goals, and 82% of all Alaska's onboard recyclables are recycled - over 1,800 tons of materials per year. Overall, Alaska and Horizon cut their per-passenger waste-to-landfill number by half since 2010 and plan to decrease it to 70% by 2020. Combined with other initiatives (such as being the only airline that composts its coffee grounds), Alaska Airlines and Horizon Air hope that less than 30% of their waste ends up in landfills. For the airline industry, this is a considerable decrease.

The Green Team has contributed to overall employee engagement, even inspiring some departments to plan and run their own sustainability-related projects. These give employees opportunities to be creative, have autonomy, and ensure that environmental sustainability at Alaska and Horizon Air is truly self-sustaining.

Drumheller shares that the Alaska Airlines Green Team "was originally formed as a way for employees who are passionate about environmental stewardship to come together and be able to work on projects to further our sustainability objectives." The group was simply something created to give Alaska's employees an outlet to their passions. While in time the efforts have benefited Alaska's bottom line, that wasn't the initial objective. "It's not as much about cost control," she explains. "These people have a job and they want to figure out how to make it more environmentally conscientious." Drumheller adds, "if people can embed environmental sustainability in their job, they feel better about their values, they're a lot more satisfied, and they feel like they're making a bigger difference."

The environmental initiatives at Horizon and Alaska not only gave employees a way to help the business but also created a cause that allowed employees to become passionate about their jobs. The Green Team's next focus is to integrate these sustainability initiatives into the practices across all of its Airbus and Boeing planes, laying the foundation for future success as the companies grow together.

Sustainability That is Sustainable
The stories of Alaska Airlines and Self-Help Credit Union illustrate that sustainability initiatives can have a profound impact on a corporation. By providing your employees with an opportunity to do something good, they become more passionate about their jobs and committed to making their company succeed. This is one of the "soft economic gains"—a change that can be easily felt, but difficult to quantify—that sustainability initiatives provide a company.

Overall, personal passion for a healthier planet is the number one driver for individuals to put their precious time and energy into sustainability initiatives in the companies they work for—either as an employee or a founder. Yet, when team members devote time to recycling efforts, create programs that encourage people to bike-to-work, or focus on saving energy, this means that time is not spent on the actual job they were hired to do. This is a challenge for management in many companies: how to find the right balance of allowing employees to spend time on sustainability initiatives that will further the innovation and growth of the company, while also ensuring that employees stay focused on their primary job functions.

An Eco Balancing Act
Dr. Bronner's, a family-owned-and-operated activist and social enterprise company that manufactures food, cleaning, and personal care products, has found a way to balance the two. The company focuses on organically regenerative agriculture, fair trade, animal advocacy, industrial hemp and drug policy reform, and fair wages (among others). One of their oldest and most profitable products is their castile soap brand, which they have produced and sold for over five generations.

Their focus on sustainability-related initiatives started in 2009 when a small group of passionate employees concluded that their mission-driven company was not doing enough with their recycling and waste management efforts. A loosely-tied group started the first informal "Green Team." Like Alaska, Horizon, and Self Help Credit Union, this informal team initiated changes that made a profound impact on the company.

Darcy Shiber-Knowles, the Senior Quality, Sustainability, and Innovation Manager at Dr. Bronner's, organized the company's first dumpster dive in 2014, so everyone involved could have a real window into the company's waste streams. In sustainability circles, a "dumpster dive" is an activity to analyze the company's overall waste output. Before this initial dumpster dive, the company's waste output and the overall environmental impact of these actions were unclear at best.

In 2014, Dr. Bronner's also published its first-ever "All-One" report. The company's website states that it is "part manifesto and part CSR report, but also so much more."5 This document contains articles written by the company's leadership and shares financial contributions of the many activist causes that the company supports. Additionally, the environmental section of the first report dug into baseline metrics around their footprint, including waste, water, electricity, and greenhouse gas emissions. The inclusion of environmental reporting in this now-annual, public-facing report is in part because of the efforts of the company's original, informal Green Team.

Based on the findings of the waste audit and the imperative of annual reporting in their "All-One" report, Shiber-Knowles began to make small changes in how the company managed waste. A team of volunteers who had participated in the dumpster dive established five separation programs for dealing with different waste components within their warehouse. Shiber-Knowles then negotiated a relationship with a recycling broker who would take the materials from the separated waste streams and recycle or reuse the material. They built on the pre-existing recycling programs, drawing ideas and strategies from the employees of nearly a dozen departments.

A year later, they repeated the dumpster dive and found that although the total volume of waste had increased throughout the company, they had reduced their waste-to-landfill output from 29% to 11%. These results created widespread enthusiasm for sustainability efforts. Shiber-Knowles remembers this win as a significant breakthrough; the yearly dumpster dive then became an exciting event for the whole company. What started out as a fun event designed to collect valuable sustainability data became a significant way to engage and educate the most environmentally passionate employees and a point of universal company pride.

In 2017, Dr. Bronner's focused their sustainability efforts in a more organized way by creating the "Green Team 2.0," the first-ever cross-departmental committee with bi-monthly meetings.

Inspired by the earlier, informal green team and positive dumpster dive experiences of employees in years' prior, Dr. Bronner's new-and-improved, formalized Green Team is empowered and revitalized. The Green Team meets regularly and builds on their past successes to reduce their environmental footprint. The goal is to drive their environmental handprint* toward a more regenerative approach, with a focus on carbon sequestration and removing waste.

Dr. Bronner's found that success in environmental initiatives requires collaboration, contribution, and cooperation from everyone. Sustainability initiatives will not stick if the entire company doesn't embrace them; one individual or department cannot be the sole driving force long-term. There was support from the highest levels of the organization, but the ideas that led to their breakthroughs and successes came from the people "on the ground," responsible for all aspects of the business. Additionally, Dr. Bronner's found that sustainability doesn't need to be burdensome to the operations of their business. Through effective organizing and planning, the company can be both sustainable and productive—and have some fun while they're at it.

Capitalizing on Curriculum
Located in New Hampshire, Badger Balm is a skincare company that produces natural sunscreen, bug repellent, and many other quality, organic products. The company became a B Corp in 2011 and used its Impact Assessment for many years before creating a Sustainability Team in mid-2015. The Impact Assessment is a tool that helps a company understand its social and environmental performance.

While leaders at Badger thought that the B Corp structure was in alignment with their mission, "we didn't have the tools or the measurement to be able to set goals internally," says Rebecca Hamilton, Collaborative Executive Officer (Badger's version of CEO, a title Rebecca shares with her sister Emily Schwerin-Whyte). The leaders set out to create a team with employees from all departments, which created less of a top-down approach to tackling sustainability matters. Their vision became even bigger as a result. In Hamilton's words, "our goal was to not only measure our impacts on a larger scale but also to educate or inspire the rest of the employees internally so that we were all more closely connected to our mission-driven initiatives."

Concurrently, Jess Baum, a graduate student at Antioch University New England, was working with a team of fellow students to develop an environmental management plan for Badger as part of their curriculum. The team conducted and reported on environmental audits for each of Badger's departments, conducted a waste assessment and provided results and procedures for potential reductions, offered a GHG assessment tool which included a methodology and information about how to use the tool for future use. The plan they composed served as a guidebook for the blossoming Sustainability Team.

As a result of this work, Baum created a full-time position for herself and is now Badger's Sustainability Manager & Community Coordinator. The Sustainability Committee she helped start is now composed of approximately a dozen employees from all departments and works with Badger's leadership on engaging employees in the company's sustainability initiatives.

Green Transformation at Genentech
The Green Genes program at Genentech, a member of the Roche group (a leading biotechnology company founded more than 40 years ago, that makes medicines for people with serious and life-threatening medical conditions) is another shining example of a grassroots movement leading to breakthroughs in sustainable business practices.

Green Genes began in 2003 when a group of passionate Genentech employees came together to lobby for compostable plates and utensils for their campus cafeterias. Together the group also took on the responsibility of "greening-up" other aspects of the workplace.

These internal efforts brought the employees' passion for environmental consciousness to the attention of Genentech's leadership team. The leadership team offered Green Genes their full support, enabling them to launch their efforts into a more formalized sustainability initiative which put Green Genes on the path to become the largest employee club at Genentech. Today, more than 4,000 employees (out of approximately 14,000) have opted to receive weekly tidbits of green wisdom through the Green Genes newsletter, and many of these employees directly contribute to the program on a daily, weekly, or monthly basis.

Green Genes made a direct impact early on. Its initial activities sparked an examination of the company's carbon footprint by the Environmental Health and Safety department, snowballing into larger projects which informed Genentech's first public sustainability goals, set in 2006.

Genentech is one of a growing number of companies that has an employee dedicated to its sustainability goals, and its large, distributed volunteer team. Katie Excoffier is the company's Sustainability Manager and has been leading the Green Genes program since 2008. In addition to serving as the president of Green Genes, she spearheads Genentech's efforts to integrate sustainability into every level of the corporation and draw engagement from all of its employees. As the Sustainability Manager, she aims to be aware of everything that is going on in the company regarding environmental sustainability. Her efforts to create cross-functional communication between department leaders and team members have been integral to the success of her role.

No One-Size-Fits-All Plan
While every company has a different story, these examples highlight the critical factors in mobilizing effective, sustainable change. The first person or group in each company took action and didn't wait for permission. Even simple, constructive steps generate excitement and community involvement, serving as stepping-stones to more significant changes down the road. As relationships grow, so do opportunities to effect change on higher levels. There is no one-size-fits-all plan. This means that you—or anyone else in your company who has an idea for improvement and a commitment to acting on, communicating, and developing that idea—can initiate these changes and more.

* Environmental handprint means "positive actions toward sustainability."

Sustainability Teams and B Corporation – A Combination for Success

Your mission-based company must be profitable to function. Owners must be able to pay those on the payroll and purchase the materials that are needed to make the products or provide the services the company sells. Insurance, healthcare, and infrastructure all factor into the company's operating budget as well. Unfortunately, the necessarily demanding focus on profit margins can cause other important responsibilities to be ignored at times.

Finding the right combination of mission and profit goals can be challenging. One of the many things that New Resource Bank, Better World Books, Dr. Bronner's, Badger, and Alter Eco have in common is that they all have B Corp certification to provide guidance and accountability in this area.

Just like other companies, B Corporations focus on increasing profits. However, the company is also dedicated to social and environmental issues. An organization called B Lab certifies B Corp companies.

Each company must meet rigorous standards focused on social and environmental performance, accountability, and transparency to achieve certification. By design, the process is not simple. For some companies, it can take months (or longer) to achieve certification.

Prospective companies start by taking the B Impact Assessment, a tool that helps assess and manage their impact on their stakeholders. Once companies earn B Corp status, they continually track their progress and measure their actions and impacts on society and the environment.

Your Sustainability Team can help your company through this process by taking responsibility for some of the data points that must be collected and measured to achieve certification. Many companies experience a disconnect between their sustainability declarations and their true measurable actions. The B Corp certification provides accountability in crossing this gap, and your Sustainability Team can be the driving force behind company compliance, as well as helping all employees understand the need and value of such a move.

Though the certification process can be arduous, designation as a certified B Corp gives businesses a healthy competitive advantage in the company's industry and also helps to cut costs as a result of more sustainable processes (many of which are shared throughout this book!). Additionally, in the 2015 Nielsen Global Sustainability Report, 66% of consumers reported that they are willing to pay more for sustainable brands—that is up from 55% in 2014 and 50% in 2013.[6]

From helping your company decrease its water and energy use to procuring sustainable cleaning products, employees on your Sustainability Teams can use their skills and green wisdom to support the company in ensuring that its initiatives are in alignment with its goals.

The following is a short interview with B Lab Standard Analyst Mike McGrory on how Sustainability Teams complement and support a company's quest to become "A Force For Good."

How can a Sustainability Team support a company in gaining and maintaining B Corp status?

B Corp certification is always a team effort. By establishing a Sustainability Team before certifying, the Environmental section of the assessment can be delegated to a group of subject matter experts. Engaging Sustainability Team members often results in a company being able to achieve a higher score on the assessment, since they are aware of their company's current practices (e.g. more efficient lighting or heating systems) and how they can be applied to certification.

Additionally, practices such as tracking carbon footprint or establishing an office composting system can be an intimidating process, but subject matter experts within a Sustainability Team can help demystify the path forward with the improvements for their company.

What step of the certification process do companies tend to struggle with the most, and how can a well-functioning Sustainability Team help to mitigate those issues?

Companies completing the assessment for the first time often score below the average score of Certified B Corps on the environmental section. A Sustainability Team can dig into the environmental section, assist in understanding the technical language within the assessment, and prioritize improvements that can be made in a short period with low to no-cost (e.g. beginning to track energy use, or developing an environmentally friendly purchasing policy).

Can you share a story or two about the practical benefits companies have experienced from their B Corp certification?

Even companies with well-established environmental practices often find new ideas for improvement in the B Impact Assessment, since the assessment represents a collection of up-to-date best practices from the B Corp community. Improvements can range from formalizing their environmental processes, to better tracking their resource use. The below excerpt about Preserve and the practical benefits they experienced from B Corp Certification is from "7 Companies Share How They Think Outside the Box to Put the Environment First" on bthechange.com, which covers examples of B Corps improving on their environmental practices.

Last year, B Corp Preserve launched a line of compostable tableware and a dispenser for our 100 percent recycled plastic cutlery. These new product lines are bringing more sustainable options to single-use products.

"Through the certification process, we were able to codify impact-positive practices that we had not formally committed to company policy. So while a lot of the things we were doing as a company were in the spirit of a B Corp, the B Impact Assessment helped us realize what we needed to commit to a written policy."[7]

How can a long-established company get over any systemic, institutional and practical barriers they might have to achieve B Corp status?

Starting the B Corp Certification process and completing the B Impact Assessment is the first step a company needs to take to move forward measuring and managing their impact for their customers, employees, community, and the environment. Check out bimpactassessment.net to start, and bcorporation.net to learn more about the global movement of people using business as a force for good.

(Thanks to Callie Rojewski for her contribution to this interview.)

Notes

1. "How Much Fuel Does an International Plane Use for a Trip?" How Stuff Works (April 1, 2000), https://science.howstuffworks.com/transport/flight/modern/question192.htm (Accessed October 3, 2018).
2. Peter Atkin, "Trash Landings: How Airlines and Airports Can Clean Up Their Recycling Programs," National Resources Defense Council (2006), https://www.nrdc.org/sites/default/files/airline.pdf (Accessed October 3, 2018).
3. Darby Hoover, "Trash Landings: How Airlines and Airports Can Clean Up Their Recycling Programs," National Resources Defense Council (2006), https://www.nrdc.org/resources/trash-landings-how-airlines-and-airports-can-clean-their-recycling-programs (Accessed October 4, 2018).
4. Inflight Recycling Up in the Air
5. "All-One! Report," Dr. Bronner's Magic Soaps (2018) https://www.drbronner.com/media-center/all-one-reports/ (Accessed October 3, 2018).
6. "The Sustainability Imperative: New Insights on Consumer Expectations," The Nielsen Company (October 2015), p. 8, https://www.nielsen.com/content/dam/nielsenglobal/dk/docs/global-sustainability-report-oct-2015.pdf (Accessed, October 4, 2018).
7. "7 Companies Share How They Think Outside the Box to Put the Environment First," BtheChange (September 26, 2017),

https://bthechange.com/7-companies-share-how-they-think-outside-the-box-to-put-the-environment-first-25bf9e8e8e4c (Accessed October 4, 2018).

* As of press time, Jacqueline Drumheller is no longer with Alaska Airlines.

2

The First Steps To Create Your Sustainability Team

Gathering the Team
It is possible that your company has at least one person eager to get sustainability initiatives underway. While one motivated person can always make a difference, facilitating the type of change you're looking for—the kind that creates and implements system-wide solutions—requires a team.

As Adam Werbach explains in *Strategy for Sustainability*, "From an ecological standpoint, few companies can 'go it alone,' regardless of their internal capacities or resources. The challenges will be too great."[1] The same is true for people. Even the best and brightest individuals need to enroll other team members into campaigns to maximize the impact and effectiveness of the initiatives. One person can be the spark plug, but never the whole engine.

This doesn't mean you should temper the passion of your sustainability go-getters. Quite the opposite! You need to build the best possible platform for that passion to spread - a Sustainability Team. Gathering smart, dedicated people to contribute their energy and share green wisdom may seem like an insurmountable obstacle, but in truth, it just takes the careful execution of a calculated strategy, a strategy that Werbach advises "must engage every part of the system—every person on staff, every supplier in the chain."

Businesses can cultivate the engagement needed to create a successful Sustainability Team by proactively offering employees the opportunity to connect their passions with their day-to-day work. According to yearlong data from 2015 Gallup polls, only 32% of US workers are "engaged" in their work.[2] The poll defined "engaged" based on employee ratings of the workplace environment, such as "having an opportunity to do what they do best each day, having someone at work who encourages their development and believing their opinions count at work."

Gallup's Amy Adkins notes, "Gallup's extensive research shows that employee engagement is strongly connected to business outcomes essential to an organization's financial success, such as productivity, profitability and customer engagement. Engaged employees support the innovation, growth, and revenue that their companies need."3 The combined total of 67% of respondents categorized as "not engaged" and "actively disengaged" represents a vast field of untapped potential and profit that Sustainability Teams can help unleash.

Regardless of company size or field of work, the chance to be a positive part of sustainable solutions is energizing and motivating to employees. Smaller companies can gain a lot of traction from the effort of a concentrated few, while larger companies will require more organizational support and team contributions to make an impact of a similar scale.

In either case, the first step towards implementing sustainable solutions is building the team that will generate them.

Keys to Starting a Successful Sustainability Team:
Enroll a few smart, dedicated people who will contribute on an ongoing basis. Find the touchpoints that generate employee participation—inspiring actions that both engage team members and educate them about important issues.

Additionally, create metrics to track all actions for every campaign you create and for every event produced. These metrics will allow you to build baselines for sustainability goals and measure the team's successes. You can then share that information with everyone involved. The saying "you can't manage what you don't measure" perfectly applies to sustainability initiatives.

Start Your Sustainability Journey Here

Many of the companies interviewed started their team by developing small initiatives that grew into extensive programs with more significant impacts. For instance, many started with a simple Earth Day event, which progressed into dealing with the company's harder-to-reach sustainability goals. Success with smaller sustainability tasks builds the foundation for a resilient team and inspires people to create larger campaigns.

Examples of "eco actions" that teams take at the beginning of their journey include:
- Printing double-sided (saving paper and ink)

- Turning off lights at the end of the work day

- Coordinating the collection of unneeded supplies for donation (such as monitors, computers, printers, etc.)

Strength-Based Sustainability

Strength-based approaches (SBAs) to social work and community development have been gaining momentum for several decades now. The underlying idea is that whether working with individuals, communities, or organizations, solutions to the deepest and most nagging problems rarely come from an external fixer's analysis of imperfections. More often, they arise out of the facilitated growth of already-present strengths.

While there are appropriate times to take a sober account of sustainability shortcomings, assembling the Sustainability Team is a great time to shift from deficit-based thinking to strength-based thinking. This means instead of asking, "what's wrong with our current processes," the team also explores, "what's right with how we're doing things, and how can we bolster those efforts?"

Employing a strength-based approach is particularly important when inventorying team resources. After all, pursuing sustainability is less about creating something new and more about rearranging what already exists into more self-sustaining cycles.

Here are a few questions that will help you take inventory of available resources, so you can start creatively repositioning the puzzle pieces:

Strengths-Based Resource Inventory

Personnel:
- Will the team consist of volunteers to achieve its goals, or can the company hire someone to manage the team's initiatives?

- Will the team members come from many departments, or only a few?

- What vocational strengths do Sustainability Team members bring to the table and how can the team leverage those strengths most effectively?

Physical Environment:
- Is the team located in an office where it can make changes to the structure, such as installing solar panels to the roof?

- What advantages or opportunities does the physical environment of the company provide?

Relationships:
- What connections do team members have to community stakeholders, sustainability networks, or thought leaders?

- Does the team have the full support of an executive leadership team, in both participation and financial assistance?

Communication:
- What are specific metrics the team can use to evaluate long-term strategies and measure those actions when they are complete.

- How will success stories be communicated to key stakeholders?

- What avenues of communication are already in place and how can the Sustainability Team use them to educate and inform?

These are just a few questions that you can use to start assessing the sustainability assets you already have and identify those that need cultivation.

Once current resources have been thoroughly mapped, the team is ready to start identifying the simplest ways to achieve results and strategizing a plan to reach each goal. Some actions will be higher priorities than others. After an initial assessment, the Sustainability Team can develop a long-term plan to reach each milestone. The team can obtain expert consultation to develop a plan, or if someone on the team has a background in sustainability, this person can guide the team through the first stages of research.

An initial strategy for the Sustainability Team is to keep the list of campaigns short and focused. This allows team leaders to gauge the team's dynamics and observe how each balances their daily, paid work with volunteer responsibilities on the Sustainability Team. During this time, team leaders can also work closely with the company's executives (more on this in chapter 3) to establish avenues of financial and directional support for the Sustainability Team.

Malkin-Weber from SHCU advises, "keep your eye on the ball. Find projects that are both meaningful and provide a payback for the organization. Sustainability Teams build their ability to impact an organization by demonstrating value and results. Also, find small but meaningful projects to do at first and then build up. It's good to get some successes under your belt."

Launch Plan Overview
Outlined below are a few of the steps needed to launch your company's Sustainability Team:

Step 1: Preparing for the First Meeting
Whether self-appointed or selected, if you are the team leader and therefore responsible for the team's efforts, be sure to have a short meeting with the sponsoring executive and encourage them to join the Sustainability Team (more on this in the next chapter). Then, start laying the groundwork for your first gathering.

- Identify one or multiple leaders who can be responsible for the team's efforts.

- Establish a regular meeting time and place.

- Invite energetic people who are excited about changing their co-workers' patterns and habits.

- Identify 3-5 potential projects that will change habits throughout the business while also saving the company money.

- Create an agenda for the first meeting.

Step 2: During the First Meeting
You're in the meeting room together for the first time. People are excited about everything they can create and improve for the company. Collaborate and take time to evaluate your target areas before you start to change the other team members' actions. Collect as

much information as possible to establish detailed baselines.

- As a group, create a team mission statement (described below). This is your guiding voice to be shared with the entire company (this task could take a few meetings, but stick with it – it is a crucial piece of the team's foundation).

- Brainstorm possible employee engagement projects and establish what will be the team's indicators of success.

- Prioritize projects based on interest or feasibility (at the start, quick, easy goals will keep the group motivated).

- Assign responsibilities to team members.

- Send meeting notes to everyone involved (especially the participating leaders from the executive team).

Step 3: Keep the Momentum Going

Consistency is key. In many cases, serving on a Sustainability Team is a volunteer role that team members take on in addition to their regular responsibilities. As a result, clear communication about the dates of upcoming meetings and milestones is incredibly helpful. Establish clear action items and communicate ways in which team members can support one another. Other steps include:

- Set a weekly/monthly/quarterly meeting time (frequency will depend on the level of resources—personnel, financial, etc.—your company can devote to the team's work).

- Continually share the volunteers' action items with the entire team to help everyone stay on track.

- Track your progress! It is vital that you see what efforts are successful and where you are making progress.

- Publicize upcoming meetings and share about upcoming events and campaigns in the company's intranet, newsletter, or other news-sharing media to increase engagement and volunteer support.

- Regularly check in with other team leaders and meet with the company's leadership team when needed.

Other Green Wisdom to Integrate Into Planning:
- Ensure that the Sustainability Team has members from as many departments throughout the company as possible (human resources, finance, communications, building operations, event planning, marketing, purchasing). It is essential to have input and

perspectives from all areas of the company to ensure successful implementation of campaigns.

- Promote the team's efforts in the company's newsletter, intranet site, or external website. In addition to spreading awareness, those who are dedicating their time and efforts to these endeavors will feel appreciated.

- Continually encourage more volunteers to join the team. This will expand the team's reach and create the possibilities for even more impact.

- Celebrate team success. Was the team's new composting process instrumental in the company achieving a massive decrease in waste output? Celebrate that! Make sure everyone involved knows that their work is vital to the company's future.

- Only commit to what is truly possible. Having too many action items in a short amount of time is a setup for failure.

Have fun! This is one of the most crucial components of building lasting change.

The Beauty of Multiple Entry Points
When employees are truly engaged in sustainability initiatives, innovation sparks and team members begin to collaborate with one another, creating cross-functional teams. This integration allows employees to understand better how the work of other

departments influences their own, encouraging future innovation and cooperation.

One of the most strategically effective ways to get a Sustainability Team off the ground is to create multiple entry points through which team members can engage, while still focusing the action on a small set of initiatives. "It's important to provide as many different entry points as possible for people to get involved into and get inspired," says Stephanie Meade, Director of Sustainability at New Resource Bank.* "People feel passionate about many different things within sustainability. One person can be passionate about animals and others might be passionate about oceans and beaches, while another is totally inspired by sustainable fashion."

Developing campaigns that attract different types of people over time is incredibly helpful in reaching a larger audience—both to enroll new volunteers, and most importantly, to continue reaching the company's goals. Meade continues, "It's all about what makes people feel passionate. I think that with more entry points focused on education through an array of initiatives, you have a higher likelihood of getting more people involved because you'll find their entry point. That has been really helpful for us."

A Team on a Mission
A mission statement will keep the team true to its established goals and help team members stayed aligned when facing tough situations. Establishing a Sustainability Team mission statement makes all departments accountable for sustainability practices and promotes better overall communication across business lines.

Your Purpose

A strong mission statement is a statement of purpose. It works best when written by the entire team so that everyone involved feels that they own it. The mission statement defines the goal of the Sustainability Team and motivates both the current members and those who aren't yet involved. Because of how foundational the mission statement is to the work of the team, it's best that this task is a high priority and starts during the Sustainability Team's formative meetings.

Get Writing!

A well thought-out and comprehensive mission statement uses a simple format to demonstrate what the team can do for the company and how it will achieve these results. This gives a team the credibility needed to gather support from other executives and employees.

While there is no prescription for the perfect mission statement, it is helpful to break it down into three parts. By utilizing the three points below, you will cover many of the practices people can relate to and work towards. This will make the structure more accessible to construct into a clear and impactful message.

Here is an example of a mission statement, using the bold words as a guide for each sentence:

- **State the aim of the team:** "We believe that sustainability is the core of effective productivity and essential for the preservation of the world's resources."

- **State what the Sustainability Team can contribute to the company**: "By implementing sustainable practices and being aware of our impact on these resources, we can make a difference. We recognize that we have a responsibility to…"

- **Finish with a strong closing sentence that encompasses the bigger vision of all activities and initiatives:** "We will produce our goods effectively, responsibly, and strive to achieve environmental sustainability in all that we do."

Adding the three sentences together produces:

> *We believe that sustainability is the core of effective productivity and essential for the preservation of world resources. By implementing sustainable practices and being aware of our impact on these resources, we can make a difference. We recognize that we have a responsibility to the environment and future generations. We will produce our goods effectively, responsibly, and strive to achieve environmental sustainability in all that we do.*

The mission statement succinctly captures the purpose of the team and the direction in which it is heading, allowing the team to build confidence and credibility in the workplace. It can be posted in visible areas to remind team members of the overall goals and serve as an open invitation for newcomers to participate.

Make Green Wisdom Accessible
The goal of creating an in-house Sustainability Team is self-sufficiency. Seeking the guidance of external consultants is a wise move, and one that will benefit you at multiple points in your journey, but the long-term goal is to rely on the skills and knowledge of your peers. To reach this point, you must invest in the growth and development of your team. Create opportunities for them to learn directly from sustainability professionals. Connect team members with the latest tools and resources, and give them a platform to share their new-found Green Wisdom with their colleagues.

Producing fun and impactful educational campaigns is the best way to engage teammates who are not involved with the Sustainability Team on a day-to-day basis. Circulating your mission statement - your shared and declared vision for the future—will build alignment and clarity so that everyone on the team (and in the entire company) understands who the Sustainability Team is, where they are going, and how they will get there.

Getting a Sustainability Team off the ground is involved, but not complicated. It starts with a single leader, or small group, gathering like-minded visionaries. As you begin to meet, develop a clear mission statement that will cast the team's vision for the company's future and keep all parties accountable. Then, inventory your resources (using the Strengths-Based Resource checklist above), and identify easy wins.

Moving forward, ensure team members have access to tools and resources that expand their knowledge of sustainable practices and a platform to teach as they learn. Producing fun, educational campaigns that also make a tangible impact is one of the best ways to onboard new team members and increase community engagement.

Salesforce: Providing Vision and Leadership to Teams of all Levels

Sunya Ojure is the Director of Sustainability at Salesforce, a position that allows her to work with sustainability-oriented teams on many levels.

The Salesforce Sustainability Team is composed of professionals whose full-time job is crafting and implementing company sustainability initiatives. For Ojure, part of that work is supporting Earthforce, one of the company's largest and most active "Ohana Groups," an internal volunteer special interest group focused on promoting sustainability and global good.

Whether she is working with her immediate team or passionate employee Earthforce volunteers, Ojure shares that it is important to clarify team priorities early on. She recommends using four key steps to focus and bring a sustainability program to maturity.

A 4-Step Journey for Sustainability Teams:

1) Seek to understand your business and how you interact with the world

Ojure shares that leaders can use these questions to gain an understanding of the team's goals:

- What is material to your business?

- What is most important to your stakeholders?

- How does your business impact the environment?

Once the team is clear on the sustainability issues that are most relevant, the team can focus on developing initiatives that make a significant positive impact.

2) Once you know your impacts, focus your work on the top 2 to 3 goals

Like at Dr. Bronner's, both the Salesforce Sustainability Team and the Earthforce employee volunteers have long lists of goals to achieve. While the potential areas of focus are positive, too many good goals can become distractions, spreading the team out so much that people feel they cannot make an impact. Creating a strategy to reach the most important two or three goals has proved most useful.

For Ojure and Salesforce, the top sustainability goals are:

- Working toward 100% renewable energy for the company's global operations.

- Continuing to deliver Salesforce customers a carbon neutral cloud and operate as a net-zero greenhouse gas emissions company.

Salesforce is a "cloud company" (a company that hosts its services online for clients to use anywhere), and as a result, its most significant direct environmental impact is the output of emissions associated with data center electricity consumption. As the leader in the industry, renewable energy and energy efficiency is a priority. Having such a focus helps to align all stakeholders and sets a sustainability team up for success. "There are a million worthy causes in this world and unfortunately we can't tackle everything," Ojure reminds.

3) Integrate sustainability into everything that your company does

A sustainability lens can be applied to all company operations. In doing so, a bridge is built between company values and employee actions. These "touchpoints" enhance employee involvement and build a stronger business.

For Salesforce, offering employees a sustainable, healthy workspace is part of their goal to advance sustainability from the inside out. In 2017, 54% of employees worked in a green building certified space.[4] The company is also striving to achieve LEED Platinum certification for its headquarters and marquee buildings, and new offices are built according to leading green building standards.

Salesforce understands that their office spaces around the world are more than buildings—they are visual representations of their company values. By creating sustainable work environments, employees, and all types of company stakeholders can physically understand how the built environment contributes to health and wellness for all.

4) Shift towards maximizing positive change

In this step of the process, the question is: "How can we have a positive impact versus just not having a negative impact?"

This may sound intuitive, but it is a crucial shift. This mentality moves businesses beyond the "low-hanging fruit" initiatives to fully integrating sustainability into their business models and cultures.

The innovative water recycling system that will be installed in Salesforce Tower is a perfect example. In collaboration with the City of San Francisco and Boston Properties, the Salesforce blackwater system will be the first partnership in the U.S. between a city government, a building owner, and a tenant to support blackwater reuse in a commercial high-rise building. The system will provide water recycling capabilities for all tenants in Salesforce Tower, not just Salesforce.

Notes

1. Adam Werbach, *Strategy for Sustainability: A Business Manifesto* (Boston: Harvard Business Press, 2009), pp. 30-31.
2. Amy Adkins, "Employee Engagement in U.S. Stagnant in 2015," Gallup (January 13, 2016), https://news.gallup.com/poll/188144/employee-engagement-stagnant-2015.aspx (Accessed October 4, 2018).
3. Ibid.
4. "FY17 Stakeholder Impact Report: Blazing a Trail Toward a Better, More Equal World," Salesforce (2017), p. 23, https://www.salesforce.com/content/dam/web/en_us/www/documents/datasheets/sfdc-fy17-stakeholder-impact.pdf (Accessed October 4, 2018).

* New Resource Bank has been acquired by Amalgamated Bank, which also has a very innovative sustainability program. Stephanie Meade now runs her own brand storytelling consulting company.

3

Getting Your Executives Engaged

Creating Maximum Potential
Many Sustainability Teams are established from the bottom-up, sparked by the passion of individual employees. This is a valid and beneficial way to begin, as sustainable shifts are often most apparent to those on the front lines. But to transition from peripheral impact to fundamental change, company leaders need to be involved. Not only can they provide the approval for significant transformations, but they can also connect Sustainability Team members to resources, champion the cause of stakeholders, and guide team ideas.

An Important First Step

"Executive Buy-In," as it is called in sustainability circles, is also necessary to validate the time and energy that your Sustainability Team members pour into campaigns and initiatives. From a practical standpoint, this means that at least one person from the executive-level (optimally, a C-suite level) of the company is willing to participate in the work of the Sustainability Team. This person has the power to allocate funds to campaigns and projects, supports your team in reaching decisions efficiently, and serves as the liaison between the team and other executives. Their participation demonstrates that the company believes the team will make a difference and is committed to the ongoing partnership.

A high level of executive buy-in makes the formation and work of a Sustainability Team more efficient. Whether one or multiple executives are involved, their role is to support the Sustainability Team with resources, help the team develop a clear action path, facilitate decision making, provide a managerial perspective, and create access to funding for campaigns and projects.

Your Sustainability Team will reach its highest potential when it has the full support and contribution of company leadership. In the 2016 Bain Sustainability Change Survey, when 301 companies were asked to name the single most significant factor contributing to the success of their sustainability programs to date, 27% of respondents named "senior leadership support."[1] That was more than double the second result, "employee engagement and interest," at 11%. "Our research," the report concludes, "shows senior leadership support is the most important factor contributing to success, and that visible actions—not words—make the difference."[2] Without executive buy-in, teams fail to gain momentum, energy decreases, and initiatives fall flat.

To demonstrate their commitment, executive teams must publicly announce their support for the Sustainability Team. This is most effective when done by the company president or CEO, as it communicates that the entire executive leadership team backs the Sustainability Team's initiatives. Additionally, this announcement makes the Sustainability Team "official" in the eyes of all employees, not just those who are actively involved. This public statement will give your Sustainability Team members the clout needed to secure support and guidance from other employees when it comes time to execute a campaign or project.

Benefits of the Sustainability Team's Existence

The support of C-level executives will go a long way towards enhancing the work of the Sustainability Team, but first, you need to earn that support. Clearly communicate that backing the work of the Sustainability Team is about more than just encouraging employee involvement. Growing an active Sustainability Team leads to a host of company benefits, both qualitative and quantitative.

Financial Benefits

Depending on your business, the financial benefits of forming a Sustainability Team are as important—or potentially more important—than getting team members involved and motivated in earth-focused initiatives. According to a study of 401 senior financial executives, up to 80% of executives are willing to forgo value-creating projects to present smooth earnings to stakeholders.³ If you can demonstrate that a Sustainability Team can create value while increasing, rather than disrupting profits, your executive will get on board in a hurry.

- **Lower costs:** More efficient processes (many of which are simple, like making double-sided printing the default setting or investing in reusable cups) lead to reduced energy and water use and fewer materials to purchase. Recycling and composting cut down on waste output and related costs.

- **Tax benefits:** The Sustainability Team can research and implement city and federal government campaigns that offer tax benefits and financial incentives for sustainability endeavors, such as installing HVAC units or energy-efficient water systems. Solar arrays, geothermal heating systems, LED lighting, and gray water systems, often have significant paybacks in addition to installation incentives. All of these save money on operational and facilities budgets.

- **Increased sales:** In 2015, sales of consumer goods from brands with "a demonstrated commitment to sustainability" posted a global growth rate of over 4%, as compared to less than 1% for those lacking such a commitment.⁴

Team Benefits

The formation of a Sustainability Team increases morale and innovation. Happy, invested employees stay with the company, decreasing turnover and saving time and money. As Alex Edmans, Professor of Finance at the London Business School, explains, "A satisfying workplace can foster job embeddedness and ensure thatalented employees stay with the firm. Relatedly, [that] job satisfaction can provide a valuable recruitment tool."[5]

Michael Lamach, CEO of Ingersoll Rand, where employee engagement scores are in the top 10% of all recorded companies, affirms the green wisdom of Edmans' assessment. "I feel certain," Lamach says, "[that] our public commitment to sustainability is a big driver of this engagement. Companies with a strong sustainability program and culture attract and retain better talent who desire a sense of purpose and contribution to a greater good."[6] He also shares that if you are looking "to connect your team's work to the global good, consider aligning your company goals to something bigger."[7]

Other advantages include:

- **Engaged staff** - employee productivity increases when team members are engaged and feel they are making a difference.

- **Hire and retain talent** - top employees want to work for innovative companies with an attractive mission.

- **Personal growth** - team members learn new, transferable skills while serving on the Sustainability Team.

Market Benefits

Authentically embedding sustainability into your business model and earning the long-term trust and loyalty of your customers are two critical components of building a successful brand. McKinsey Global reports, "Year over year, large shares of executives cite reputation as a top reason their companies address sustainability."[8] In fact, of the 13 core values they polled in their 2014 survey, top executives "say reputation has the most value potential for their industries. However, many . . . respondents [also] say their companies are not pursuing the reputation-building activities that would maximize that financial value."[9]

Other factors include:

- **Increased market** - commitment to high environmental, social, and governance (ESG) standards leads to higher market shares and higher visibility of the company brand.

- **Reduced risks** - unsustainable actions create strategic and operational risks. The Sustainability Team can help mitigate those.

Importance of Building the Business Case
To earn executive support, your company's Sustainability Team leader will need to demonstrate the company's need for the proposed initiatives. The team must build a data-driven business case that highlights potential cost savings and brand improvement, using examples of successful actions taken at similar companies. Developing this case as a team serves multiple purposes. It forces Sustainability Team members to research and relate best practices of industry leaders, become proficient at quickly explaining the value the team creates and lays the groundwork for successfully onboarding company executives.

How to Build the Business Case
When building the business case, start with your final product, and then work backward. The goal is to create a proposal that will describe the mission and work of the Sustainability Team, outline the benefits that work will produce, and describe the steps involved in accomplishing the proposed goals.

While one or two people will need to be in charge of the final assembly and polishing, the background research can (and should) be divvied out among Sustainability Team members so that all contributors take ownership in the final product and have an increased knowledge base as a result of the work.

The Proposal
The following is a template that your team can use to outline a proposal to present to the Executive Team:

- **Overview:** draft a short synopsis of the team's mission and purpose (this can include information about current challenges).

- **Benefits:** determine and demonstrate both quantitative and qualitative benefits for the company as a result of the Sustainability Team's actions.

- **Expenses:** develop a bulleted list of all expenses, with a short, one-sentence explanation for each as needed.

- **ROI:** explain cost savings over time (show timeline and savings).

- **Risks:** outline the risks of the Sustainability Team (give a holistic picture of all actions and demonstrate how the team will mitigate each item).

- **Measure:** share how the team will measure campaigns and initiatives.

- **Report:** demonstrate how team success will be reported to all stakeholders.

The more detailed your team's proposal, the better. Executives want to see a clear plan that demonstrates how the team will be organized and how campaigns and events will be executed. A slide presentation can work just as well as a PDF proposal as long as both meet these guidelines. Go ahead and take some time to determine the best way to communicate with the executive in question and develop your proposal accordingly.

Level of Executive Involvement
The role of the executive on the Sustainability Team will vary by company. Discussing the level of executive involvement is an important conversation during the initial formation of the Sustainability Team.

Some companies involve upper management sporadically to preserve the grassroots energy of their Sustainability Team. In these cases, executives have a hands-off approach and allow the Sustainability Team leadership to advance initiatives themselves, providing mentorship, resources, and access to financial support only when asked.

Other companies take a more formal approach to the Sustainability Team, inviting executives to participate in every decision and campaign. These executives are incredibly active and attend all meetings. They serve as the liaison between the Sustainability Team and the other executives, provide crucial support to the Sustainability Team leaders through one-on-one meetings and conversations, and can even act as the "spokesperson" for the Sustainability Team's efforts to the entire company.

Increase Overall Engagement
Mountain Rose Herbs (MRH), a producer of organic spices, herbs, and teas, is an excellent example of a company that has a strong link between their Green Team and the executives. The MRH Green Team is a voluntary group that strives to promote environmentally and socially conscious practices by reducing waste, conserving energy and water, encouraging alternative transportation, and informing and motivating co-workers about

workplace giving and volunteer opportunities. Regarding the executive buy-in at MRH, Alyssa Bascue, Director of Sustainability, shares:

> *"I think that it's crucial to have that top-down influence. We are a very bottom-up and grassroots company and we have an open door policy where all employee[s] can come and make a suggestion. Shawn Donnille is one of the owners of Mountain Rose Herbs. He joined the Green Team about a year ago (in 2016) and it has been extremely helpful having a top decision-maker there with us. He not only answers questions that employees may have, such as "what's the history of our waste policy?," but he is also there to explain the reason why we haven't implemented specific programs or suggestions. He can have that direct communication and I know that a lot of our Green Team members feel very lucky to have those one-on-one conversations with him."*

Like the executives at Mountain Rose Herbs, those at Dr. Bronner's are integrally involved in the work of the Green Team. Shiber-Knowles shares:

> *"The Bronner and Milam families support environmental initiatives 150 percent. One example of what that support looks like is from a past dumpster dive. Our 73-year-old CFO, who is a Bronner family member, was*

one of our divers. I can't imagine that happening many places, but she was right alongside a junior employee from the shipping department picking up garbage and putting it in the right bin and recording the weight of the waste. Her service wasn't about glamour, and it wasn't about the photos. It was because she really cares and because she wanted to learn about our waste streams and be a part of our efforts to improve. Her time out there during the dive was a message of authentic support, which is one of the ways I know that we will be successful in our initiatives."

"It's really important to have that voice of leadership in the room with us," reaffirmed Baum, Badger's Sustainability Manager. "I think that without having at least one of them in a meeting it would be hard to feel like we're getting things done." Two of the company's family-member owners are on the executive team and are instrumental in ensuring that actions within the Sustainability Team move along effectively.

Baum shared a similar story about how family members at Badger were instrumental in supporting the team's decrease in company waste output. In 2014, the company's waste output was 72% (meaning only 28% of their waste output was recyclable or compostable). In 2017, "we are at only 5% waste-to-landfill, which is a direct reflection of leadership buying in and creating excitement around making an impact," says Baum. Having a mobilized and energized Sustainability Team combined with a passionate leadership team is a winning strategy for companies that want to reach their sustainability goals.

When owners or executives are fully engaged with the Sustainability Team it positively impacts the level of employee engagement ensuring that they feel their voice is being heard and their actions are necessary.

Sharing Green Wisdom Makes Initiatives More Effective

Salesforce, which produces the world's leading customer relationship management tool, has an incredible amount of executive support from its founders, which is an excellent asset for Earthforce. The 7,000-member group has volunteer liaisons in offices all over the world, and the top-down support of the team's efforts has a far-reaching impact on the company.

But the executive commitment to sustainability extends beyond supporting volunteer movements like Earthforce. Since day one, Salesforce founders have been vocal and passionate about integrating social impact into the company's business model, dedicating 1% of employees' time, 1% of its technology, and 1% of company resources to make the world a better place. This has become known as the 1-1-1 model.

"Our leadership sets the tone," says Ojure, Salesforce's Director of Sustainability. "We're really fortunate that we have a culture of social impact at Salesforce," she reflects. This values-based culture fosters greater cross-functional collaboration, which is key to the success of sustainability initiatives.

The Sustainability Team's close connection to leaders throughout the business helps ensure that there is buy-in and alignment. "We have a sustainability review board, which is a group of executives that we check in with regularly," Ojure says. "There are executives from many core partnership areas such as real estate, procurement, general operations, and marketing. This strong connection and support help make the team more effective."

Strong Executive Support is a Priority
When a CEO, founder, or another high-level executive also serves as the spokesperson for the Sustainability Team it shows that the company is serious and committed to the sustainability goals. Attention from even just one high-level executive can set the tone and the pace for your team, supporting you in reaching your milestones and serving the environmental interests of the company.

Whether the executive supporting the Sustainability Team dives in or stays hands-off, it is important for this executive to understand and support the team initiatives, spearhead funding needs, and develop a strong connection with other executives. All the Sustainability Team's efforts can be lost if the executive team does not allow or support the team's actions.

The extent of executive buy-in and involvement in a company's sustainability initiatives helps define all of your Sustainability Team's endeavors. While executives do not necessarily need to be involved on a daily basis, successful teams make an effort to include senior management in their work as much as possible. Developing a data-driven plan focused on deliverables, milestones, and expense-saving initiatives is an excellent way for you to introduce executives to the work of the Sustainability Team in terminology that they can immediately appreciate. Helping upper-management understand how these efforts will make a long-lasting and valuable impact on the company is one of the most important steps you can take to see your Sustainability Team blossom.

Dumpster Diving Creates the Connection

Sustainability is deeply entrenched in the DNA of Dr. Bronner's, even though the company only recently created their formal sustainability team. The dumpster dives that inspired their Green Team have proven to be effective in creating a company-wide sense of community.

"At Dr. Bronner's we are lucky to work for committed visionaries—radical, generous, and practical people who want to use this business that they've inherited from our founder as an engine for positive change," says Shiber-Knowles, Senior Quality, Sustainability, and Innovation Manager at Dr. Bronner's.

It is clear that the executives at Dr. Bronner's are "walking their talk"—using their support of the Green Team to build congruence between the ethics and values of the company and its daily practices. Their involvement demonstrates that they are committed to driving change within the company. By participating in company-wide activities—especially ones that might require getting their hands a little "dirty"—they get a close look at the places that the company can improve its waste output processes.

Shiber-Knowles continues, "When I originally proposed that we would do a dumpster dive as part of our waste audit, I thought it would be bold to set our goal of zero waste to landfill before we even count the waste. That's bold for a manufacturing operation of our size that doesn't really know what's in our waste streams."

However, when Shiber-Knowles shared this audacious goal with the CEO, David Bronner, he quickly said, "Yeah, absolutely!" A classic photo was taken of Bronner at the dumpster dive event, sitting cross-legged inside a bin of separated recycling materials with his arms raised up into the air and a big smile on his face. After the event, the CEO opened an employee meeting by celebrating the dumpster dive and giving kudos to his mother for participating. "To say that we have executive support for these initiatives is an understatement," Shiber-Knowles concludes.

Notes

1. Jenny Davis-Peccoud, Paul Stone, and Clare Tovey, "Achieving Breakthrough Results in Sustainability," Bain & Company (November 17, 2016), https://www.bain.com/insights/achieving-breakthrough-results-in-sustainability (Accessed October 3, 2018).
2. Ibid.
3. This study was referenced on p. 28 of Adam Werbach's *Strategy for Sustainability*. John R. Graham, Campbell R. Harvey, and Shiva Rajgopal, "Value Destruction and Financial Reporting Decisions," *Financial Analysts Journal* Vol. 62 (6) (November 2006), p. 33, https://www.cfapubs.org/doi/pdf/10.2469/faj.v62.n6.4351 (Accessed October 4, 2018).
4. "The Sustainability Imperative: New Insights on Consumer Expectations," The Nielsen Company (October 2015), p. 2, https://www.nielsen.com/content/dam/nielsenglobal/dk/docs/global-sustainability-report-oct-2015.pdf (Accessed, October 4, 2018).
5. Alex Edmans, "The Link Between Job Satisfaction and Firm Value with Implications for Corporate Social Responsibility," *Academy of Management Perspectives* 26(4) (2012), p. 2, http://dx.doi.org/10.2139/ssrn.2054066 (Accessed October 4, 2018).
6. Michael W. Lamach, "How Our Company Connected Our Strategy to Sustainability Goals," Harvard Business Review (October 27, 2017), https://hbr.org/2017/10/how-our-company-connected-our-strategy-to-

sustainability-goals (Accessed October 4, 2018).
7. Ibid.
8. Sheila Bonini and Anne-Titia Bové, "Sustainability's Strategic Worth: McKinsey Global Survey Results," McKinsey & Company (July 2014), https://www.mckinsey.com/business-functions/sustainability-and-resource-productivity/our-insights/sustainabilitys-strategic-worth-mckinsey-global-survey-results (Accessed October 4, 2018).
9. Ibid.

4

Make Your Approach Unique

Building A Custom Plan
Every company has a unique energy, culture, and set of values that inform company life and work. Some businesses offer employees paid time to volunteer or work with Sustainability Teams. In this structure, the time spent on these initiatives occurs during regular work hours, not before or after. Other companies creatively incentivize volunteer work. Some integrate work on sustainability initiatives into an employee's yearly review.

For example, when an employee spends time on a Sustainability Team initiative that serves the entire company, such as a composting campaign, she may not be directly paid for her time, but the work is recognized by earning additional points toward a favorable yearly review. At times, some companies also reward time spent on sustainability initiatives with awards or financial bonuses.

The reality is, great ideas come from passionate employees, not because they are incentivized with awards or money, but because they are genuinely dedicated to leaving a smaller environmental footprint and desire to create a more harmonious connection between their work and values. Still, these incentives can provide appropriate opportunities to honor the effort of employees and volunteers.

Strategies for Effectiveness
The Sustainability Teams represented in this book have surpassed the status of "grassroots efforts." The teams and their initiatives are now deeply rooted into the fabric of the business model. They contribute to cost savings in energy and waste reduction and attract and retain talent. The leaders involved know that the upfront investment of time and resources will pay off with increased savings and sustainable practices in the long run.

This integration can be seen in the work of Self-Help Credit Union's Environmental Stewardship Committee. The committee is project-focused, and their actions reflect their mission and function within the company.

For example, many of the committee members work on the Commercial Lending Team. Their work often includes financing clean energy projects for their clients, and as a result, they are incredibly knowledgeable about clean energy and the policy involved in this ever-changing industry. Self-Help's Real Estate Team collaborated with these in-house experts for advice on adding a solar array to the rooftop of a commercial office building.

To leverage the human capital they already possess, Self-Help takes on environmental sustainability efforts at the level of each business unit, allowing team members to operate out of individual strengths and maximize the effectiveness of each project. Where possible, volunteers enjoy working across silos. For instance, Environmental Stewardship Committee members collaborate with Workplace Wellness volunteers and property management staff on wellness challenges in which teammates from locations across the country compete with each other to take the stairs instead of the elevator.

Levels of Engagement
Like New Resource Bank, Genentech offers their employees numerous opportunities to engage in sustainability initiatives, including lunch-and-learns, movie nights, field trips, and beach cleanups. Some members stay updated on the latest green wisdom by reading the monthly Green Genes newsletter, others attend events regularly, and some become leaders of sub-teams to work on specific initiatives.

Sustainability Manager Katie Excoffier is experienced in developing strategy and goals, and collecting, analyzing, and reporting data to support these goals.

By providing oversight to the volunteer program, she ensures that there is continued momentum and allows the Green Genes volunteers to focus on their day jobs. Her role and abilities complement the work of Green Genes and add value to the entire company by synthesizing the work of the company's Sustainability Council with that of the Green Genes subteams and campaigns.

At Genentech, communication processes are also crucially important, both to foster collaboration among those who serve on the Sustainability Council and to ensure that employees are aware of all the sustainability efforts and Green Genes initiatives. During each monthly Sustainability Council meeting, there is time allotted for the Green Genes team leaders to provide ideas that have come through the employee suggestion box. This direct communication pathway is integral to Green Genes' success.

A Top-Down and Bottom-Up Approach
Genentech's Sustainability Council works with Green Genes to further the company's sustainability initiatives. The Sustainability Council is comprised of six Steering Committees that are accountable for specific sustainability areas—Energy, Water, Waste, Transportation, Wellbeing, and Green BioPharma—and who work with Green Genes volunteers to create programs and monthly campaigns focused on these themes.

The governance structure is modeled in such a way that Green Genes is plugged into the Sustainability Council, which is composed of program managers whose day jobs focus on various areas of sustainability. Each program manager leads a cross-functional Steering Committee, including a volunteer Green Genes subteam leader from various parts of the organization.

Genentech has a "bottom-up and top-down" structure, which contributes to efficiency and progress. (Image provided by Genentech.)

The Sustainability Council's Energy Steering Committee exemplifies this structure well. The Green Genes volunteer subteam leader regularly collaborates with the Energy Steering Committee members. Together, they plan employee engagement programs and create campaigns that encourage team members to reduce energy use and contribute to the overall Green Genes mission. This coordinated action bonds corporate work with volunteer endeavors and creates a seamless foundation for green wisdom sharing.

An Effective Multi-Tiered Approach
Better World Books (BWB) is a for-profit social enterprise and online bookstore that collects and sells new and used books online, matching each purchase with a book donation, Book-for-Book.™ BWB sources books from thousands of libraries, colleges, and other sources in over half a dozen countries. Those books are then sold and shipped to over 200 countries.

According to Dustin Holland, Vice President of Global Sales and Marketing at BWB, the company recently reorganized the structure of their Sustainability Council. The council has evolved from a command-and-control operating system (which provided needed operational structure and drove change from the top-down) to an adaptive operating system (in which operational structure is already in place, and the members of the Sustainability Council are empowered to drive improvements to the Company's Sustainability mission and focus energy on high-impact projects). This transition has proven to be a more efficient way to operate, as it decreases the time spent implementing projects at multiple facilities and increases employee engagement in the company's sustainability mission, which is what matters to BWB's stakeholders.

Their ten-person Sustainability Council is sponsored by a member of the executive team (this is Holland's second role at the company and demonstrates stellar executive buy-in) and led by a member of the leadership team. The council is comprised of people from all practical departments in BWB's four physical locations (plus remote workforce) and represents broad interests, skill sets, and backgrounds. "We embrace individuality across the company, and let our teams shine," Holland shares. The voices of those from the operations and logistics departments are crucial and have proved to be valuable in supporting the company to analyze their processes to decrease energy and resource use. Holland sums the council's goal up nicely: "We are committed to ensuring that we collectively work together in a coordinated fashion to make the biggest impact for our stakeholders (including the planet!) with the resources available to us."

Like many other people who serve on Sustainability Teams, those at Better World Books are volunteers who put in time outside of their day jobs. Council members meet in the morning before their workday starts and perform the necessary tasks on lunch breaks or after work. However, due to the global composition of the team, those on the council meet at various times throughout the month. Early morning meetings help to maximize their time together and avoid distractions. "This is extra work so that weeds people out. Only the truly committed make the time to attend these meetings and get things done! It's not a social group," Holland says.

Style Affects Structure
According to Holland, ensuring that the team is comprised of a variety of different leadership styles is an essential factor in maintaining motivation. "The real key is to examine who is on the team and make sure that you have doers, instead of only people who are simply passionate about the environment," Holland says. As a result, BWB has created a vetting process for individuals wanting to join the group to ensure that everyone on the team is up for the task. The roles are important and contribute to the company's mission and bottom-line, so candidates who desire to join must be sponsored by their immediate supervisors. "From there, adds Holland, "it's more about the team members coming up with ideas and executing them, and me supporting them in terms of getting resources allocated so they can pull off whatever it is that they want to accomplish."

Collaboration is Key

Out of approximately 200 employees, fourteen participate in the new-and-improved Dr. Bronner's Green Team. "It's important for us to be driven by collaboration," says Shiber-Knowles. "As a manufacturing entity, we require everyone's cooperation and contribution. If sustainability initiatives are just being driven or implemented by my department, they're not going to succeed, and they're not going to last."

At Dr. Bronner's, the structure of grassroots, bottom-up development is key to successfully implementing their vision and mission. "When I look back at the success that our Green Team-like initiatives have had over the last four years," Shiber-Knowles reflects, "it's been the ideas that have come from the specific departments where those ideas have been implemented that have been the most successful."

When team members bring sustainability challenges and want to brainstorm solutions during a Green Team meeting, they might think the issue affects only them, or only their department; however, it is possible that those in other departments are experiencing the same sustainability issues as well. As Michael Lamach, CEO of Ingersoll Rand, notes:

> *"The best opportunities for improving the environmental impact of an organization come from the people who are closest to the day-to-day mechanics, and shortcomings, of existing procedures. They are often the first to recognize and raise up areas of*

improvement, and it's important that leadership is ready to listen.

Too often, however, the employees who are best positioned to influence change do not understand how they can contribute or may not view sustainability as a business imperative."[1]

Creating a place for people from many different functional areas to come together, share ideas, and collaborate to develop solutions, facilitates positive change.

At Dr. Bronner's, there is a three-step process to turn Green Team ideas into realities that the executive team will support. First, team members bring ideas to Shiber-Knowles, in or out of scheduled meetings. "It's my job to make sure those ideas get championed," she says. Tangibly, championing those ideas means ensuring that executives and owners know what is happening within the Green Team conversations, as well as advocating for funds if financial support is needed for a project idea. Lastly, she communicates the project ideas externally, "so we can report on it in our All-One Report." Sustainability ideas, she reiterates, "need to come from the people who are doing the work." This structure of creating solutions through collaboration on multiple levels is beneficial for the Dr. Bronner's team.

Creating a Climate Fit for Life
Sustainability is the focus for all employees at Interface, the world's leading supplier of modular carpets. Mikhail Davis, Director of Restorative

Enterprise, shares that at Interface, everyone in the company functions as part of the Sustainability Team. "Whether you're on the R&D team developing far-reaching things that fundamentally change our processes, for example, to reduce the amount of heat we need, or you're on the Operations Engineering team figuring out how do we make the ovens we have today run more efficiently, you're on the Climate Action Team," Davis says. This unified mentality is critical in bringing about Mission Zero—a goal that has been guiding Interface's sustainability work since 1995.

Mission Zero is Interface's pledge to eliminate the company's negative effect on the environment (including the climate) by optimizing all of its business processes by 2020. Mission Zero "is our promise to show that businesses can make, what our founder Ray Anderson called, 'a bigger, better profit' by learning to operate within the limits of the biosphere," says Davis. Everyone at Interface is focused on how the company can be profitable without having a negative, hidden backstory about the impact of the materials and processes used to make carpet tile. The team is dedicated to demonstrating to the world that it is possible to run a business—even a global, for-profit business—in a way that actually makes human and ecological life better rather than worse. "This starts with taking responsibility for the truthful impact of the company," Davis asserts.

"Climate Take Back" is Interface's mission beyond 2020. It is a framework for creating a future climate that is "fit for life," rather than solely focusing on limiting the damage done by climate change. The idea is that by being optimistic and hopeful about future possibilities, companies can focus their efforts on transforming their industries through innovative solutions. "First and foremost, we want to contribute and change the conversation around business and climate from 'being less bad' to taking the lead in solving the big challenge civilization faces," says Davis. All team members at Interface contribute to this mission, and Davis hopes that more businesses will join in on the efforts to "get us back to creating the climate we want, rather than one that we all might survive."

The Problem is the Solution

One of the challenges Dr. Bronner's has faced in implementing the new Green Team initiatives is that hourly employees have to step away from their work responsibilities to participate in Green Team meetings. While the time commitment of serving on the Green Team poses a challenge for their salaried employees, when an hourly employee attends a Green Team meeting, the entire production, warehouse, or shipping team they are a part of has to figure out how to cover that share of the work and ensure that operations can continue smoothly.

The easy solution would have been only to allow salaried employees to serve on the Green Team, but Dr. Bronner's was committed to diverse departmental representation. To help solve the problem, the company executives agreed to bill the hours that Green Team members spent meeting and working on projects to the Sustainability Department. Additionally, the Green Team shifted their meeting schedule to work around the times when different departments need all hands on deck for daily operations, and the team made sure there were tasks that team members could accomplish outside of meeting times if there was a workflow conflict.

These intentional logistics, although requiring a bit more coordination, allow both salaried and hourly team members to equally participate on the Green Team without adversely impacting their departments. Now the Green Team encompasses employees from almost all departments, creating a more cohesive, holistic approach. Everyone can contribute their valuable insights, and the hub-and-spoke communication model provides sustainability feedback to all departments from designated Green Team representatives.

One department cannot be responsible for all that it takes to ensure that an entire business is sustainable, and Dr. Bronner's has a particularly big list. "We want to get to near zero waste to landfill; we want to reuse our wastewater, we want to eliminate our greenhouse gas emissions and eliminate food waste. We also want to sequester carbon on the premises in the future through the application of compost generated onsite to a small orchard that provides fruit for employee consumption," Shiber-Knowles says. "These are audacious goals and it's going to take everyone's ideas and participation to make it all happen. Working together will advance our "All-One" culture."

Everyone at Dr. Bronner's—from warehouse workers to the family members who were born into the business—knows that the company will not reach its sustainability or impact goals unless everyone works together as a unified team. "We are facing the climate crisis as a global community," notes Shiber-Knowles. "If you take a moment to consider how to address climate instability, you'll see that it's going to take everybody."

Green Wisdom Ambassadors

While Mountain Rose Herbs' Green Team has volunteers from many departments, a vast majority are from customer service—people who process phone or online orders— and the shipping and warehouse departments. Team members from both the shipping and warehouse departments have key roles in the company's overall sustainability campaigns and make important contributions to the company's Green Team.

With around 150 employees in the company, the dozen that serve on the Green Team are "eyes and ears" for Director of Sustainability Alyssa Bascue. They participate in the monthly meetings, learn about campaigns, and share announcements, then take the information back to team members in their own department, where they serve as ambassadors for the company's sustainability initiatives. As a result, Green Team ideas and campaigns are threaded into departmental conversations and policies. In turn, Bascue serves as an ambassador for the Green Team. She has a document that defines the MRH Green Team and she freely shares it with anyone who is interested, promptly answering all questions and providing information about participating in the group.

Volunteers Integrated into Sustainability

Like Genentech, the volunteer-driven Earthforce team at Salesforce is integrated into the Corporate Sustainability Department, an impact-focused group whose executive reports directly to the Salesforce

CEO. This department sets Salesforce's environmental strategy and oversees many initiatives, such as employee engagement, using Earthforce as its primary method of engaging employees. Specialists in the Corporate Sustainability Department work on areas that are material to the business model, such as event sustainability, green building programs, renewable energy, data center and infrastructure, strategy and executive engagement (all of which are crucially important to a cloud company like Salesforce). Company-mandated sustainability departments that focus on corporate social responsibility reporting or obtaining government energy rebates combine well with the actions of volunteer-led affinity groups.

Aviation Company Commits to Sustainability
Of approximately 21,000 employees, 270 are on the Alaska Airlines "Green Team News" newsletter mailing list, and fifteen are actively involved in the Green Team's activities. Many more participate in one-off events, such as brown bag lunches, workshops, or volunteer opportunities.

Like Dr. Bronner's, Alaska Airlines established a framework so that team members know how much time they can focus on Green Team activities while "on the clock." Some employees whose work focuses on sustainability also engage in Green Team activities, making it challenging to discern if their activities are considered volunteer time or work time. This can create a blurry line for these team members concerning responsibilities and roles.

The Alaska Airlines Green Team was created to raise awareness and gain resources for "green" topics. "Our

Green Team focuses more on employee engagement and getting people involved in our sustainability programs rather than focusing on specific tasks or projects," says Jacqueline Drumheller, Alaska's Sustainability Manager. Big initiatives will come with time. Right now, "we're trying to get more people into this sustainability plane," she adds with a laugh.

Though the focus is on engagement, Drumheller shares that "The Green Team is very active. With the millennials coming in (as a result of the acquisition of Virgin Airlines) there's a lot of excitement about the Green Team and so we're getting a lot of fresh blood." Participating on the Green Team, Drumheller continues, is "a great way for people to collaborate and meet others who have the same sort of inspiration and initiative from departments all over the company—people from maintenance, from in-flight, and more; not necessarily people who have the opportunity to talk to each other."

While Alaska Airlines (a transportation company) and Dr. Bronner's (a soap and impact company) couldn't be any more different regarding their products, their use of Sustainability Teams to bring people together from all over the company is almost identical.

For Drumheller, having people from all parts of the company involved in the work of the Green Team contributes to a deeper understanding of sustainability issues:

This way you learn so much, you learn about every part of the organization. You get to every single corner of the company. It's like being responsible for sweeping a giant warehouse. You're going into all the little corners where you never noticed there was stuff going on before and getting familiar with them. I don't think you can learn more about a company than being involved in sustainability or being on a green team because you get to examine everything and see what makes the company tick.

While Drumheller acknowledges that the division of labor of sustainability initiatives shared by the Green Team and the corporate side can be unclear at times, she still believes they can be complementary. "The Green Team was created to raise awareness and get out and make the business case [for sustainability]," she says, "while the corporate side is to create visibility for the Green Team. It's morphed over the years and a lot of people who are on the Green Team also have sustainability as part of their job description."

Ingrained Focus on Doing Good
Stephanie Meade of New Resource Bank shares that NRB's mission is to "achieve well-being for all people and the planet." This is unique for a bank!

While the bank provides similar services as other financial institutions, the way it operates on an internal level sets it apart. Meade explains, "We have this really deep culture of sustainability. For us, it comes internally. It starts with all the practices we have in place as a company and the Green Team is kind of a holder all of these practices. The Green Team is like the 'embodiers of the mission.'"

Always thinking critically about what well-being of people and the planet truly means, the Green Team focuses on sharing their green wisdom through sustainability initiatives and education (more on this in Chapter 7). Over the course of the year, they actively welcome employees to participate in their Sustainability Engagement Program, Earth Day celebration, orientation for new employees, and their waste diversion practices.

Formats are Flexible; Collaboration is Mandatory
Sustainability Teams fit into company structures in many different ways—from volunteer-only groups coming together to have fun on Earth Day to company-directives that are tied to employee's yearly reviews. Though not always the case, team structure is frequently more complex and integrated with larger companies and more loosely-tied and informal for smaller companies. Regardless of structure, it is clear that effective and useful sustainability programs cannot be run from just one department. It is important that at least one person from all departments participates on the sustainability team.

This cross-functional approach helps to improve communication and collaboration among people who do not usually work side-by-side. There is no foolproof solution for organizing Sustainability Teams; the same structure will not work for all types of companies. However, with the support of company executives and the creation of a well-thought-out plan that facilitates effort and dedication across departments, a Sustainability Team can soar!

A Different Approach to Sustainability Efforts

Focused sustainability teams don't work for every company. Nutiva, a company that consciously curates non-GMO, organic superfoods (such as coconut oil, hemp, chia, and more) is an excellent example of combining form with function. Gretchen Grani, Nutiva's Director of Sustainability and Social Responsibility,* is solely responsible for ensuring that all sustainability initiatives are carried out and align with the company's bigger vision. She works closely with the heads of all the business units to gain support and "human power" to bring the initiatives to life.

However, Grani didn't start with this position. Initially, Grani was hired as the Director of Administration in Corporate Giving; most of her job responsibilities focused on ensuring that the company's move from Southern California to Northern California went smoothly. She naturally gravitated toward implementing sustainability initiatives in their new office, and one of the first things she did was to choose recycled carpet, no VOC paint, and energy-efficient appliances. With a lot of effort on Grani's part, Nutiva became a certified sustainable business through the California Green Business Network. At this point, she realized that developing a sustainability department was necessary for the company's evolution.

Grani researched and wrote a proposal sharing that the company was ready to increase the effort and energy it was devoting to sustainability initiatives. She believed that integrating more sustainable systems and processes into the company business model would allow Nutiva to walk its talk even more. The proposal encouraged all company players and stakeholders to engage the initiatives at an even deeper level (even more executive buy-in). "First of all, sustainability contributes to the positioning of the brand," she explained. There are also cost savings achieved through sustainability which contributes to the resiliency of the supply chain."

After becoming the Director of Sustainability, Grani pitched the executives another proposal: strategies for Nutiva to become a zero waste company, which she based off a handful of best practices achieved at another company in their industry. "I don't think any Sustainability Director has it easy," Grani reflects. "All of us have to be well-versed in making the biggest business case, well-versed in being persistent and well-versed in influencing and persuading others."

When Grani accepted the role of Director of Sustainability, she decided to dismantle the company's Green Team. While she was successful in creating a business case for sustainability and persuading the executives at Nutiva to build her ideas into the business model, she "found that it was very cumbersome to work as a team." Though she wanted to facilitate collaboration, "My initiatives are very fluid, so I found it more effective to have smaller meetings and interactions, rather than work with a large group."

My work is based on one-on-one partnerships with different heads of each department. For example, I am partnering with the Head of Distribution to evolve our transportation systems to be more efficient. I am partnering with the Head of Social Media to tell our story. I am partnering with the Head of Maintenance to do an energy audit. I am partnering with the Head of Purchasing to find out how we can be more efficient in our packaging.

Grani's streamlined approach may seem counterintuitive to some, but it allows her to move quickly and efficiently, while still encouraging collaboration and receiving input from all areas of the organization. Her results speak volumes!

Notes

1. Michael W. Lamach, "How Our Company Connected Our Strategy to Sustainability Goals," Harvard Business Review (October 27, 2017), https://hbr.org/2017/10/how-our-company-connected-our-strategy-to-sustainability-goals (Accessed October 4, 2018).

* As of press time, Grani has a new position at Guayaki Sustainable Rainforest Products and is now the Regeneration & Sustainability Cebadora.

5

From Breakdowns to Breakthroughs

Declaring the Intention of the Team
You can show true courage by stepping up and declaring the need to start a Sustainability Team—especially if your company does not currently emphasize caring for environmental and social issues. Your independent vision and awareness are what is needed to shift the status quo and begin to move toward a more sustainable future.

Effective communication skills, the ability to create relationships, trustworthiness, and commitment are all characteristics that are incredibly important to leading a volunteer-based team. Each of these traits helps enroll other team members into the cause and keep people motivated.

Breakdowns as Interruptions
In *Language and the Pursuit of Happiness*, Chalmers Brothers describes a "breakdown" as "an unexpected 'break' in the normal flow of what I was doing, in the normal routine of my day."[1] Although "Breakdowns may initially seem to be all 'negative,'" he writes, "they are not positive or negative in and of themselves."[2]

More specifically, Brothers recognizes breakdowns as "unexpected interruptions in the fulfilling of a commitment." If that commitment is to your next sip of coffee, a breakdown may not be very notable; but for many sustainability leaders and teams, the commitments they have made to far-reaching sustainability milestones and goals, not to mention their commitments to stakeholders, customers, and the environment, can make breakdowns seem like true catastrophes.

In the business context, breakdowns affect all departments, even when the most polished processes are in place. Many leaders interviewed for this book experienced different levels of breakdowns within their Sustainability Team as well. Breakdowns occur regardless of the experience, connection to resources, and overall commitment of the group. Even well-funded sustainability teams with a high level of executive support experience times when team members disagree or commit their attention to other parts of the business, interrupting the fulfillment of their public commitments.

For the most part, Sustainability Teams are composed of voluntary groups of people with full-time jobs, complete with daily deadlines and responsibilities. As a result, challenges both big and small will occur as the team navigates its way through communication snafus, decreases in momentum, differing expectations, budget cuts, and even employee turnover.

To be successful in the long run, team leaders need to share and manage expectations, so everyone is clear about their responsibilities. Clearly communicating expectations will foster compassion when a plan changes (especially due to "day job" responsibilities) and create consistency for meetings and events so that people can plan accordingly, and the team can continue to move toward its goals.

There are many ways that Sustainability Team leaders can re-inspire, reignite, and regain trust and momentum when things don't go as initially planned. Your strong leadership in these times of "interruption" can be the catalyst that turns a breakdown into a positive breakthrough in team communication or processes.

Market Force on Recovering from a Breakdown

According to Tony Cooper, CEO of Market Force, a training program used by innovative organizations to advance human dynamics, all teams and projects have breakdowns. Cooper agrees with Brothers and says that "breakdowns are inevitable. They are anything that gets in the way of what you wanted to have happen. However, a breakdown is only a temporary stop and an opportunity for learning."

In a revelation of true green wisdom, Cooper shares that being upset about breakdowns is similar to being upset about the weather. For example, say your Sustainability Team leaders create the expectation of hosting an Earth Day event at a local park. One team member orders delicious food, another invites community partners, and on the morning of the event, everyone arrives at the park early to prepare. However, ants begin to crawl all over the food. There is construction across the street that is louder than the music from the speakers. Then, clouds roll in and begin to dump rain. Your long-awaited Earth Day event breaks down.

"It's not a personal attack on you or the team," Cooper shares, "it's simply an occurrence in the world. But because there were an aspiration and an intention, and because the Sustainability Team wanted something to go in a particular way, and now that the world is not going that way, it is seen as a problem." Cooper points out that breakdowns are ultimately defined by intention. Fortunately, realizing this allows your team the opportunity to recommit to your core intentions and adjust expectations accordingly.

The core intention of the Earth Day event was not to eat good food, listen to music, or enjoy a sunny afternoon—though all these might be valid expectations. The core intention was to connect, educate, and further the team's mission. Fully committing to your core intentions often requires adjusting your planning to ensure core success, even if that means sacrificing some of your secondary expectations.

If, for example, your Sustainability Team had planned the Earth Day event inside the local community center instead of outside at the park, poor weather would not have caused a breakdown because the team strategically prioritized intention over expectation. Or, if the intention was for the Sustainability Team to bond by putting on its first event, the rained-out picnic may have provided a memorable opportunity to connect and converse with team leadership under a soggy park ramada.

In this case, having an intention for the team (or event) is similar to writing a collective mission statement that binds the team to a shared vision for the future (see Chapter 2 for support with a mission statement). Ideally, when individuals work together to create a shared reality, they stay focused on the bigger picture—the specific goal or milestone they are working toward and why they are working towards it. Reconnecting with that mission shifts the focus away from the breakdown and toward the team's original intention. This decreases the negative attention on why things aren't working as planned and refocuses that energy on how the actual reality can contribute to the goal.

"A team has to have a shared intention to begin the journey to ensure everyone is on the same page so that it can efficiently recover from breakdowns," says Cooper. "Otherwise, the team will just focus their work on the wrong things. The team will then become its own breakdown, and unfortunately, it will become an unresolvable breakdown." However, he encourages, "when a team is committed to its intention, no obstacle will ever stop it."

This intention-driven mindset gives you and your team the resolve needed to overcome obstacles, as well as the ability to be flexible when expectations are not met. Cooper acknowledges, "We never start a journey knowing how we're gonna get to the end. Ever. We make a lot of assumptions, we think we might know, but you know the journey is really good at instructing us about how the world is or what the paths toward success look like."

The following stories share how these sustainability leaders transformed a break in action within their Sustainability Team into a learning experience that sparked new actions and opportunities to thrive.

Overcoming Time Challenges
Time management is often at the root of Sustainability Team breakdowns. When a team is composed of people who contribute their time on their lunch hour, or before or after work, the time spent on the affinity group is precious. "One of the biggest challenges is that we airlines are very lean organizations and everyone is extremely busy with their day jobs," says Drumheller of Alaska Airlines. "Most of the Green Team members are management employees, not those on the 'front lines.'"

One of the easiest ways to keep people involved and motivated is to ensure that tasks are evenly distributed, so nobody feels overwhelmed by their Sustainability Team responsibilities. For example, the "YES" culture of Dr. Bronner's is the secret to their success, yet "on the other side of the coin, it is one of the big challenges in our fast-paced culture," says Shiber-Knowles. The company has executive support for their Green Team 2.0 and often a budget for their initiatives; and, like many Sustainability Teams, their volunteers have a long list of potential projects that will save the company resources and money while increasing morale. But, at the end of the day, even the Green Team 2.0 has a limit to what they can realistically accomplish.

"We can't say yes to everything and that's one of the challenges that we face. We have finite resources in the day," adds Shiber-Knowles. "We can make big improvements with the low-hanging fruit but getting the last 2% of the bigger sustainability endeavors complete will really provide us with the most challenges."

To mitigate breakdowns and burnout, here are some ground rules you can keep in mind when developing your overarching plan:

- Schedule only 1-1 ½ hour (maximum) time windows for monthly meetings.

- Divide the roles and responsibilities, so everyone has bite-sized chunks of action items to complete between meetings.

- As the team leader, communicate with team members between meetings through email (or better yet, take a few moments to stop by the desks of the key players and have a quick check-in).

- Understand that at times, the "paying" job of the teammates comes first, and volunteer actions come second.

- See how you can support those on the team with resources, such as more information or connections to other people in the company who can help team members achieve their goals.

- Prioritize what is most important for the entire company (see below).

At times, just being a leader is challenging. "It's really tough." Drumheller shares, "On one hand, I want people to pursue their passions and put their energy into something meaningful." But, she adds, "there are times when team members want to pursue initiatives that aren't specific to the business model or do not have meaning to the organization." This is challenging on a personal level since she would like to support everyone in pursuing the causes that are most important to them.

Taking Responsibility for Breakdowns
Breakdowns can also occur when a team creates goals but does not reach them. To combat this, Dr. Bronner's is intentional about avoiding a culture of blame to facilitate growth and learning within their team.

"We actually didn't improve our waste diversion in the last year, which we learned at the last dumpster dive," Shiber-Knowles recalls. However, after not reaching their zero waste goal, the team was more energized than ever to analyze their processes further. "We had a great talk about why that was," she continues, "and then a team member, who is not in management, created a winning solution for our challenge" (the solution is shared in Chapter 9). The breakdown, when handled constructively, inspired a positive solution that will have long-lasting effects on the company.

When beginning the conversation about how to improve their processes in the future, the group made a conscious decision not to focus on what had occurred in the past. "That's not resilience; that's better than resilience," Shiber-Knowles exclaims. She and her team are dedicated to supporting the company in becoming "anti-fragile, or regenerative" so that it can be even more resilient and continue to be a leader in its industry. This core intention protects the team and all its members in the event of a breakdown. Similar to the Market Force approach, the team's shared mission encourages members not to dwell on failure and to view setbacks as learning lessons for the future.

Reigniting Momentum with a Clear Plan
Maintaining a clear mission (as described in Chapter 2) maximizes your team's effectiveness. Momentum decreases when it is unclear what the team—or even the company—is working towards.

For Rebecca Hamilton and Badger Balm, one of the most important parts of building a capable team and presenting a clear mission was clarifying individual roles:

> *"From a leadership team perspective, the biggest struggle was at the beginning when we were trying to figure out what the purpose of the Sustainability Team would be and how it interacts with people's day-to-day role in their department. For example, at Badger, it is not the role of someone on the Sustainability Team to research fair trade sources of ingredients for their products, as it is the responsibility of an individual who specializes in this area (usually Operations or Product Development) to find sustainable sourcing options. However, members of the Sustainability Team are responsible for educating and inspiring everyone in the company about sustainable sourcing through engagement campaigns and events."*

Everyone on the team is a valuable contributor because everyone has different (clear!) roles. With Baum and Hamilton's oversight (in addition to Katie Schwerin, Badger's COO, Co-Founder & Co-Owner), the Sustainability Team at Badger formed subcommittees and completed the easier action items first. The additional fine-tuning allowed team members to make a meaningful impact while still balancing their workloads. "It's a really powerful team that can do a lot and has been really inspiring to the rest of the company," Hamilton adds.

Yet, even with the strategic adjustments, after the initial burst of energy among the group, the momentum faded. "There was a stopping point where everything was paused," Baum recalls. After many important strategy sessions, the team created a yearlong engagement program focused on sustainable sourcing—the company's overall focus for the year. (Read the end of Chapter 6 for more information about Badger's year-long program.)

As with many large campaigns focused on the environment, Badger started the program with a big Earth Day event and a week of awareness events. "All of a sudden we had all this heart and excitement and people were really wanting to do things that make a difference," Baum says. While the team always had a clear vision and a positive outlet for employee energy, their organized and collaborative approach in engaging employees through their Sustainability Committee's year-long initiative elevated this outlet and amplified the energy.

The yearlong employee engagement program was successful, however, "at the end of [the program] we had another "what's next" moment and we realized that we didn't have a long-term impact plan. What we wanted is to have a net positive social and environmental impact on the world with mission-aligned and science-based metrics that we can track over time," Baum explains.

As a result, Baum, Hamilton, and Schwerin collaborated to create that long-term impact plan and propose it to Badger's Board of Directors. The final result provides a framework for all of their actions, ideas, and future initiatives. It also brings energy to all team members and connects everyone to the company's mission-driven values, defining their focus and articulating the difference Badger wants to be in the world (also, the plan is constantly evolving!).

Finding Green Wisdom on the Front Lines
In addition to time and communication challenges, operational processes can also lead to breakdowns. Many logistical and operational processes depend on each piece performing perfectly so that the "whole" functions smoothly. If one piece of the puzzle breaks, the entire puzzle is broken.

Having people on the Sustainability Team that are "on the front lines" is especially important in larger companies. Leaders from Better World Books, Dr. Bronner's, and Mountain Rose Herbs have all found that the team members experiencing unsustainable practices within their role or department are often the individuals who inspire the most change and create the most effective solutions.

"We look beyond the low-hanging fruit and find things that are out of the ordinary to fix," shares Holland of Better World Books. "For instance, our forklift drivers are in the warehouse almost 24 hours a day, 7 days a week. One operator realized that they were going twice the distance necessary to deliver a product, using twice the amount of propane needed." The Sustainability Council helped develop new, more efficient forklift routes that saved fuel, time, and money.

Another Better World Books Sustainability Council member helped optimize the company's packaging machine to avoid wasteful packaging and excess shipping costs. Relying on those who experience the day-to-day processes to bring both problems and solutions to the attention of the Sustainability Team helps increase the company's ROI. "This [contributed to a] huge savings when you look at things like this, especially in a business where every penny counts," confirms Holland.

Bring in Fresh Perspectives

Breakdowns aren't always about the flow of operations. They can also occur when team members have lost motivation or feel stuck in a rut.

If your events are feeling monotonous, or everyone is focused on a challenging work milestone, energy for Sustainability Team activities will wane. To remedy this situation, you can easily bring in some fresh energy and new perspectives to help those in the trenches stay inspired.

When Alyssa Bascue of Mountain Rose Herbs (MRH) wants to motivate the Green Team, she starts with herself. Before she can be a cheerleader for her team, "[I] make sure I am inspired and do my job well," she says. When motivation does decrease, she takes an action-oriented approach to getting everyone back on track. One of her favorite ways to do this is by inviting guest speakers to share their insights and green wisdom with the entire team. In the past two years, MRH has hosted three speakers from the local area: Northwest Center for Alternatives to Pesticides, Beyond Toxics, and McKenzie River Trust.

"It was helpful to break the routine of our normal agenda" she recalls. "We would have a normal agenda at our meetings, ensuring that everyone shared departmental news and gave folks updates about where we were with our zero waste certification."

These updates could take over 30 minutes of a 60-minute meeting. For team members not involved in these details, the lengthy review might kill their motivation to attend future meetings. Focusing on initiatives that involve all team members, such as an educational speaker, or community outreach campaigns, will keep everyone engaged and energized.

Drumheller employs a similar approach at Alaska Airlines. "Sometimes what I like to do is bring in a Green Team leader from another organization, or a related organization, such as Expedia, so she or he can come in and give us some examples of what they are doing within their organization. This inspires everyone and re-energizes them to focus on the campaigns that are meaningful for the organization."

Communication is Key
Bascue also experiences challenges when the MRH Green Team is working at maximum capacity and does not have the bandwidth to focus on a great idea or project suggested by a teammate. "How do I then communicate that back to the team and make sure that they're not getting discouraged?" Bascue questions. "I want everyone to continue to bring me these ideas, and I want them to know that they are heard." While they may not be able to act on the initiative right away, she doesn't want to take the wind out of her team's sails.

Bascue has found that clear communication is crucial in moments like these. It is her responsibility to know the limit of what her team can realistically accomplish while also maintaining an energetic vision of what they might be able to do in the future. Bascue is aided in this by the strong executive support she receives from company co-owner Shawn Donnille. He attends many of the sustainability meetings and is incredibly helpful in answering questions or discussing why a campaign can or cannot be executed.

When Melissa Malkin-Weber runs into similar problems at Self-Help Credit Union, she falls back on simple, time-tested communication practices. "If there appears to be a misunderstanding, I avoid email whenever possible and I pick up the phone and call people," she says. "This way you can hear what's really going on in somebody's mind and learn the story or the motivation behind their concern." Overall, "paying attention to communication" is most important for Malkin-Weber.

Here are a few other simple tips to support stronger communication as the team leader:

- Send meeting agendas in advance—prepare all information a few days before the meeting, post it on the company intranet for everyone to view, and email it directly to all those on the sustainability team.

- Ensure that everyone has access to past meeting minutes—again, post to the company's intranet, and send directly to those on the sustainability team. This makes information available for all team members, including management and those who weren't able to attend the meeting.

- Have two team leaders responsible for a group of people or a project—this way, if one is sick or busy with work, the other can ensure that the project plan continues. It also supports continuity in the event of a personnel transition.

Humans Are Not Perfect
Generating company awareness of the importance of a Sustainability Team is a huge first step. If your business is ready to launch a Sustainability Team, that is an accomplishment worth recognizing, in and of itself. The team will make mistakes, but these experiences will help create future resilience—an important trait as the environmental landscape for business evolves.

While Dr. Bronner's hasn't reached their sustainability goals yet, it is possible that the new Sustainability Team 2.0 will push them to 100% compliance. To prevent discouragement about setbacks along the way, Shiber-Knowles emphasizes continuous improvement and humility, reminding everyone to focus on building the kind of world they all want to live in. She sums up the Dr. Bronner's approach to challenges nicely: "We acknowledge we're not perfect; we acknowledge we're human; we acknowledge we work with machines that break; we acknowledge that people get sick and people have bad days. So perfection is not the goal, instead, growth and improvement are the goals."

Cooper of Market Force agrees. "Perfection is never the outcome we seek. It's the experience. Breakdowns are normal things that occur in the world but they only impact us when they get in the way of us wanting to achieve what we want to achieve."

Building Resilience for the Future

Breakdowns can occur on account of faulty logistics, poor communication, or when the responsibilities of team members' paid positions make it impossible to focus on other areas of interest. As a leader, you must stay focused on the Sustainability Team's mission and intention. Learning how to avoid breakdowns, as well as how to move through them and prevent similar setbacks in the future, is crucial to the team's long-term success. Using the skills necessary to overcome challenges and learn from even the smallest setbacks can make a positive impact on Sustainability Team operations, enabling team members to work more effectively and support the company in reaching its goals.

When a Sustainability Team can move through challenging situations, find solutions, and continue striving toward a shared goal, it becomes a resilient and invaluable asset to the company. "Most people say that breakdowns are the best thing that ever happened to them because it got their team thinking in a different direction and opened their minds," says Cooper. "People will share stories with examples that describe how a breakdown resulted in saving a ton of money, time, or other resources. So, breakdowns always end up offering some wisdom and value."

Re-inspiring the Team

Especially early on, it can be challenging to understand all that is required to reach set milestones clearly. As a result, some teams declare goals that they do not reach which can negatively impact team momentum. Yet, even in the midst of setbacks, a few healthy conversations and productive action steps can realign everyone with the group's mission and encourage all members of your team.

Here are a few ways to re-inspire your Sustainability Team after a setback to ensure team members will continue dedicating time and energy to your crucial initiatives:

1) Celebrate even the smallest victories
Changing the habits and patterns of entire groups of people is not an easy task. Attitudes don't change quickly, and the pace of the Sustainability Team might be different than the pace of the company. Serving as the group responsible for promoting these important changes can be daunting, especially if there are resistant team members. Congratulate everyone for their efforts in achieving small milestones and celebrate bigger wins as they come.

2) Acknowledge breakdowns, then move on
During weekly or monthly meetings, focus on a breakdown for a set amount of time. Then, complete the conversation and move on. "One thing that separates truly successful people is understanding that there will always be headwinds and there will always be challenges," says Tony Cooper. "Those are not problems—those are pathways to the solution." Take note of what happened, and use the experience as a lesson on how to approach future campaigns or initiatives.

3) Publicize the team's efforts
Share all successes with everyone on the Sustainability Team, with everyone at the company, and even on the company's website. People love to learn about success stories. Your success story could be the inspiration that other companies need to reach their own sustainability goals. Even small celebrations can be shared with the world for everyone to learn from.

Notes

1. Chalmers Brothers, *Language and the Pursuit of Happiness* (Naples, FL: New Possibilities Press, 2005), p. 203.
2. Ibid.

6

Connecting To The Community

The Ties Between the Company and the Community
Your business has the power to make huge, positive impacts in your local community. Whether by developing initiatives that decrease the company's contribution to local landfills, organizing events to collaborate with community members, or cleaning litter along nearby trails, the Sustainability Team can strengthen the connection between your company and those who live nearby. The formation of a corporate Sustainability Team demonstrates your company's commitment to making the community a

healthier, greener place to live and sends a message that the business is an active part of creating a sustainable future.

Those who participate on Sustainability Teams do so because they care about how they spend their time. They want the company they work for to be better for the planet in the future than it was in the past. They think about climate change and know that businesses influence consumer behavior. People like knowing that the company in which they invest their time and talent is making a positive local impact.

Getting in the Dirt
The Sustainability Team can develop the campaigns, programs, and events that bring together people from all departments within the company. Developing public, sustainability-related engagement programs, such as beach cleanup days, Earth Day festivities, and other educational events, is a useful and fun way to build long-term connections between the company and the community.

The Green Team at Mountain Rose Herbs (MRH) is incredibly effective at strengthening ties with their local community. They do this by focusing on the natural environment of Eugene, Oregon, where the company is based. Green Team members regularly partake in restoration projects, such as removing invasive species and planting native trees.

Through the efforts of the Green Team and other employees, MRH carries out six to twelve restoration projects each year. Working with state agencies and local, non-profit organizations that are dedicated to the environment, Green Team members work hand-in-hand to ensure that local streams and wetlands are functioning as nature intended. In 2017, MRH:

- Led 12 local environmental restoration projects
- Engaged 432 community volunteers
- Logged 1,786 volunteer hours
- Removed 385 gallons of trash
- Removed 12 cubic yards of invasive plants from local riverbanks
- Planted and mulched 265 trees and native plants

Their Green Team was instrumental in these important events. "It's a great way for people in different departments to get together, get outside, and get their hands dirty," Bascue says.

Raising Awareness for Herbs
Creating events that attract people outside of the office walls allows you to deliver valuable information to community members while also informing potential customers about the types of products and services your company has to offer. Delivering sustainability information through fun, interactive, and engaging themes will have a lasting effect on those who participate.

With heavy lifting from the marketing department and their proactive Green Team, MRH organizes "The Free Herbalism Project." The event is a public venue for thought-leaders to share their green wisdom about plants and herbs. Herbalists from all over the country travel to Eugene to speak about their area of specialty. In 2016, well-known herbalist Guido Mase and ethnobotanist Susan Leopold shared their plant wisdom with hundreds of attendees. The "Free Herbalism Project" allows the community to benefit from this knowledge and publicly demonstrates MRH's commitment to environmental stewardship. By selling t-shirts, books, herbs, and other specialty items at the event, MRH raised $1,400 for United Plant Savers, a non-profit that protects medicinal plants in their native habitat. In 2017, over 1,000 people attended the bi-annual event.

Spreading Green Wisdom
By supporting other companies as they launch their Sustainability Team, or serving on the board of a local non-profit, your members can contribute to other organizations that have similar missions. These are also valuable ways to learn what other companies and organizations are working on and bring that information back to your Sustainability Team.

Bascue spends time serving on a handful of local and regional trade associations focused on herbs in the state of Oregon. This involvement allows her to learn about both the significant changes and the subtle nuances of the sustainability landscape. Through meetings and conversations, she shares the best practices and challenges facing MRH, helping other companies learn from their efforts. Bascue is also active in other natural food-oriented organizations. From 2013 to 2016, she served on the board of the Willamette Valley Sustainable Foods Alliance, a regional association composed of companies that promote natural food, and is still an active member. Bascue also serves on the membership committee of the Provender Alliance, a group that provides education, leadership, and tools for the natural foods community.

Books as Gifts

Dustin Holland of Better World Books (BWB) shares that the mission of spreading literacy and education is central to BWB's operations. Rather than allowing this commitment to remain a secondary pursuit, they use it as the driving force behind their sales and growth. A more successful company means greater mission impact and vice versa. Of course not every sustainable initiative translates to profit, but Holland recognizes that even those that don't, ultimately bolster the company's mission and contribute to their overall success. This is clearly demonstrated in the pride surrounding BWB's book donation program. "It's one of the most valuable pieces of the business," Holland says. "Although it doesn't generate revenue, it's a whole lot better than having to recycle books." To start, the company procured a book donation mobile—that despite being well over 10 years old, had only 20,000 miles on it—from a local public library. "We repurposed it and now we go out in the community and donate books to kids, and we go to senior homes and give them large print books to read. This is very rewarding for everybody involved," Holland says.

Everyone is an Ambassador for Change

Once you and your fellow team members start to learn about the small ways in which you can make an impact on climate change, you will want to learn even more and share that green wisdom with the other people in your life.

Shiber-Knowles sees Dr. Bronner's Green Team members as "Sustainability Ambassadors" to each of their respective communities. "Within the movement to address climate instability and other environmental challenges, we know it's going to take everybody," she says. "We have more than 200 employees here at Dr. Bronner's who I believe are ambassadors within their families and in their communities outside of work. Change first happens at an individual level, and then individuals change the lives of those around them." In Shiber-Knowles' view, the Green Team is not only beneficial to the company, and in the bigger picture, it makes a positive impact on society. Other individuals and companies in the global community will take notice of best practices, implement similar practices into their lives or programs, and be a part of the change in business.

Paid Volunteer Time in the Community
Some companies offer team members paid time off to volunteer, which provides Sustainability Team members the opportunity to contribute to community or environmentally-focused events. Marc Epstein, Distinguished Research Professor of Management at Rice University and author of *Making Sustainability Work,* notes that such actions can lead to additional benefits as "Organizations also have found that employees involved in company-sponsored volunteer programs report, on average, higher levels of satisfaction, increased enthusiasm for their jobs, and lower turnover rates."[1] Companies of all sizes can design a program that allows team members to take time away from their daily responsibilities while still being productive and effective in their day-to-day roles.

Salesforce encourages all employees to volunteer in their local community. The global company offers 56 hours of paid volunteer time each year to all its employees. This gives Earthforce volunteers, as well as all Salesforce employees, the opportunity to make an even more significant impact outside of the walls of their offices. Similarly, Mountain Rose Herbs offers employees 24 hours of paid time to volunteer on social, environmental, or community causes.

Embedding Community Service into All Positions

A crucial role of any Sustainability Team is to provide sustainability-related information to other team members, helping them to further enhance their roles and responsibilities as environmental stewards. This support can lead to exponential levels of impact if those other team members work directly with people in the community.

For example, team members on the Environmental Stewardship Committee at Self-Help Credit Union regularly distribute green wisdom to colleagues on their team or in their office location. This information helps employees at all levels integrate sustainable practices into their roles and responsibilities.

At Self-Help, these efforts are guided at every level by its mission to "create and protect ownership and economic opportunity for all."

> *"We do this by providing responsible financial services, lending to small businesses and nonprofits, developing real estate and promoting fair financial practices. While our work benefits communities of all kinds, our focus is on those who may be underserved by conventional lenders, including people of color, women, rural residents, and*

*low-wealth families and communities."*²

Each Earth Day, everyone on the staff can participate in a tangible activity, such as weeding at a local teaching farm. They also seek to deepen the understanding of how environmental stewardship connects to the company mission. Malkin-Weber explains, "when I talk to my teammates about saving energy or conserving resources, I make sure to connect the dots with how environmental sustainability supports our mission. For instance, energy efficiency is not just about reducing our power bills—it's about reducing the impact of fossil fuel pollution on low-income communities. Those impacts start with mountaintop removal mining in Appalachia, and lead to well-water pollution from coal ash storage across the Southeast. In between, there's mercury pollution and asthma from burning coal. These are real burdens for the communities we serve."

To embed programs directly into staff members' lives, the Green Team at New Resource Bank organizes annual and quarterly volunteer events. The annual event takes place during the week, and the four quarterly events take place on weekends. Volunteer events include organized beach cleanups, urban tree planting, clothes sorting at Goodwill, and other inclusive programs. Meade shares, "the focus of volunteering is less about learning something new, [and] more on giving back and being active participants in our community."

A Yearly Financial Contribution
Sustainability Teams can also research and identify non-profit organizations for the company to support through yearly financial commitments or specific fundraising campaigns.

In 1999, Nutiva committed to dedicating 1% of annual sales through its foundation to organizations that advance sustainable agriculture, donating $4 million to many organizations since inception. While the Nutiva Foundation recently shuttered, the company continues to donate funds that promote sustainable agriculture and the growing of healthy food within their business communities.

While this is not necessarily a Sustainability Team initiative, it is an incredible way that a leading food company gives back, not only to their local community but also to the communities that are a part of its supply chain. Sustainability Teams at other companies can use this program as inspiration to create similar company-wide programs by aggressively pursuing the ever-important executive buy-in.

Skills and Passion Used to Strengthen Links
Your Sustainability Team has the power to create unique, thoughtful campaigns that give back to your local community. At the outset, team members can focus on easy-to-attain goals while you determine what approach works best with your company culture. The impact can be large or small—what is most important is that people bring their skills and passion together to reduce the company's climate impact and create a stronger link with community members.

As you dream about the potential impact of your Sustainability Team, let your clearly-crafted mission statement and the needs of your local community guide your thinking. As these examples demonstrate, the campaigns, programs, and events your Sustainability Team coordinates are unique opportunities to establish your company as a leader in local sustainability efforts. Take advantage of the opportunity these events provide to showcase your company's services and products, but also remember—the primary goal is education and relationship building. Using the vital work of your Sustainability Team to promote inter-departmental relationships and develop community partners will produce long-lasting benefits for your business.

Community Engagement Menu

Building a successful event can be an intimidating task, so use the following "menu" as a guide to make your planning easier. Choose an event type, identify the location, then add community partners and educational aspects, and voila! The Sustainability Team will help create a strong connection between the company and its community.

Event type

- **Education** - think speakers, workshops, demonstrations, and fairs. Educational events will likely be in one location and focus on awareness and information transmission. Invite a thought leader for a specific talk or workshop, and focus on a specific theme; or, create a fair with booths and invite community partners to share their information.

- **Action** - talking about making a difference doesn't need to take the place of making one. Wear your work clothes and get dirty with these potential projects. All of them provide plenty of time for one-on-one conversations. Brainstorming and debriefs can happen over lunch breaks. Make sure volunteers are working with people outside their own department. Also, the more executives you can get in the mud, the better!

- **Reactive** - remove non-native plants that might be causing harm to other plants in the local area, organize a highway cleanup, restore a local waterway, plan a fun dumpster dive or create a recycling sorting event that is brings people from all departments together.

- **Proactive** - plant trees! Get your hands in the dirt and start forging a company legacy that will grow with your business. Design a rain garden for the community, plant trees, landscape with native plants, install a medicinal herb garden along the outside of your building. The possibilities are endless.

- **Field Trips** - tour a LEED certified building as a company and discuss practical possibilities for green architecture, geothermal heating, solar arrays, and more over lunch.

- **Celebration** - good work deserves recognition. Follow the example of companies like Genentech and throw a Sustain-a-party. The best part is that celebration and education aren't mutually exclusive. Creative twists like local food spreads, bike-powered mixers, and solar-fueled fun ensures that your party is also informative and restorative.

Community Partners

- **Agricultural Extensions** - an excellent resource for learning about composting, community gardening, soil testing, and more. Provide the space for workshops on tree pruning, beekeeping, or other activities of interest.

- **Goodwill** - facilitate a company-wide clothing swap and have a Goodwill truck on hand to accept donations.

- **Adopt-a-highway** - check out the website to learn how to take responsibility for local roadways while also advertising your business to millions of drivers (www.adoptahighway.com).

- **Local Farms** - be the entry point for employees and community members into the local food system.

- **Sustainable Businesses** - no one is asking you to put a spotlight on your competition, but invite other local business who are making positive strides in sustainability. Have a solar-powered landscaper demonstrate their products or a local apiary hand out honey samples.

Location
- **Company** - hosting the event on company property can bring awareness to your services and space, generating valuable community contact. Bonus: it's free!

- **Community Event Center** - shared public space can be an excellent option for educational events, like hosting a thought leader or sustainability fair. If your community doesn't have an event center for rent, think about where your local farmer's market meets and use that space if available.

- **Park** - spending time in a natural environment is the single best entry point into the work and conversation of sustainability. For an urban setting, rent a ramada at a local metro park. For a more rural option, consider the same at a state park. Both provide opportunities for an educational native plant or ecology walk.

- **Local Farm** - farmers who are doing things the right way love to get people on their property. Set up an educational tour and let them do the planning for you, or rent or barter for space on the farm for the day. Even if your event has a different focus, the setting will be a learning opportunity and get attendants thinking about the local food system.

Make It Fun
- **Music** - break out the speakers, or better yet, invite an up-and-coming local band. Remember every aspect of your event is an

opportunity to collaborate and build relationships.

- **Games** - don't make it all business. Even at an educational event, make sure there's time for conversation and community over a game of cornhole.

- **Raffles** - everyone loves freebies. If you have multiple tables or events, have attendees get signatures from each table to qualify for a sustainability-focused prize. It will encourage engagement and add to the festive atmosphere.

- **Food** - the key to every successful event. Skip the packaged cookies and pizza and keep the fare fresh, fun, free, and local.

Clearly, these ideas are just the tip of the iceberg. Don't worry about making every event perfect—start by just making them happen. As you move forward, remember that every logistical challenge is an opportunity to think differently, challenge norms, and highlight the innovative spirit that sets your company apart!

Notes

1. Marc J. Epstein and Adriana Rejc Buhovac, *Making Sustainability Work: Best Practices in Managing and Measuring Corporate Social, Environmental, and Economic Impacts* (San Francisco: Berrett-Koehler Publishers, Inc, 2014), 2nd ed., p. 55.
2. "Our Mission," Self Help Credit Union, https://www.self-help.org/who-we-are/about-us/our-mission (Accessed October 8, 2018).

7

Benefits of Participation

Education Through Engagement Programs
Sustainability Teams are no different than other types of teams. All participants will have different levels of experience, awareness, and skills. The team needs only one person to take initiative, which will then provide many other people the opportunity to share their wisdom.

While people may be at different places along the path toward sustainability, all types of green knowledge can contribute to the Sustainability Team. For example, a team member might have a thorough understanding of her city's recycling program and want to help implement a similar initiative at your company. Another could have many years of volunteer experience with a non-profit solar company. This person might take the initiative to bring her solar awareness to the Sustainability Team and help implement a solar project on the business roof. Whatever the case may be, allowing people to share their skills, ideas, and thoughts will maximize the team's positive impact.

On a personal level, learning more about sustainability practices and initiatives can be a significant career boost for everyone on the team. Sustainability-oriented collaboration helps employees gain a better understanding of the inner-workings of other departments, increases their interaction with executives, and adds new skills and qualifications to their resume.

Other benefits of participating in a Sustainability Team include:

- **Elevating Your Profile** - joining the Sustainability Team facilitates connections with people outside of a specific area or department. The most effective teams are cross-departmental—stakeholders in all areas of the business come together to develop initiatives. These partnerships provide employees with opportunities to gain a deeper understanding of company operations and offer insight into areas that can be improved. When an individual grasps the company's bigger picture, they can more effectively advance that vision. The work of the Sustainability Team can be a natural setting for this growth.

- **Gaining New Skills** - as part of a Sustainability Team, members attain skills that their day job may not afford them. They will have opportunities to lead meetings, organize campaigns, or spearhead relationships with sponsoring executives. This type of education, which allows employees a safe environment in which to grow leadership, goal setting skills, and overall confidence, is an incredibly valuable asset to the company and individuals alike.

- **Learning Through Shared Purpose** - people everywhere enjoy the sense of belonging that comes from pursuing a common goal. Learning about sustainability issues, especially those that impact daily life, brings a sense of collaboration and cohesiveness. A significant portion of life is spent at the workplace: make those hours count. Developing campaigns and programs that bring team members together and instill a shared sense of purpose will enhance members' lives, inside and outside the office.

Sharing the Knowledge
There are many opportunities for your Sustainability Team to create educational programs for its own team members or the company as a whole. These programs

can focus on more significant picture sustainability issues, such as global climate change, or smaller, more focused aspects, such as installing energy-efficient light bulbs in common areas. Regardless of individual backgrounds, every team member will gain valuable insights or new perspectives through these worthwhile initiatives.

Highlighting specific, eco-related educational themes is a valuable way for the Sustainability Team to share their green wisdom with the rest of the company. In April of 2017, Earthforce reached thousands of people in their San Francisco office through their promotion of Earth Month. Activities offered throughout the month included movie screenings, expert speaker talks, Earth Day celebrations, and volunteer events with local nonprofits. These themes and activities can be easily replicated by companies of any size to attract people with different interests.

Let's Do Lunch
"Brown Bag Lunch" events are very popular and serve as an excellent way for people to come together and learn about specific topics that influence company practice and private life.

The format of this type of gathering can vary widely but is most successful when it engages company culture. While some companies provide a catered lunch, others might serve drinks and ask the team members to bring their own food to enjoy. The team leaders who host the event organize the theme and invite a knowledgeable speaker to share their green wisdom.

New Resource Bank hosts monthly gatherings called "Lunch & Learns." At the beginning of each year, the team outlines a macro theme for the year and then tries to breakdown that theme into months. All Green Team activities and sponsored events engage the current theme. For example, during the "Climate Change" month, the team invited a climate scientist to present his findings and explain the data people often hear in the news during the Lunch and Learn event.

The Environmental Stewardship Committee at Self-Help Credit Union also enjoys learning from outside experts at Lunch & Learn events. "The hook is to have a speaker from the outside who is working on something interesting, which then builds the internal conversation that we can carry on in an email afterward, or distribute documents with ideas," Malkin-Weber says. She shares that while the organization has staff throughout the United States, she tries to increase accessibility by using video conferencing, allowing co-workers from other locations the opportunity to watch remotely.

Speakers from like industries are often invited to speak during the Brown Bag Lunch events at Alaska Airlines. Drumheller, Alaska's Sustainability Manager, shares, "one month, we had a representative speak from REI (Recreational Equipment, Inc.) about their Green Team programs." Another month at Alaska, the focus was on solar, and the team members learned about something that they could implement in their home lives: how to get solar panels on their home roofs to save energy and money.

People love when they are offered different topics, or "entry points" (as Meade from New Resource Bank recommended in Chapter 2) to learning. This also helps interest a diverse group of people. Be creative! There are so many sustainability themes that appeal to a wide audience for these educational lunches. The trick is trimming that list to only twelve topics per year!

Deeply-Embedded Programs
In 2014, McKinsey & Company published the results of their "knowledge collaboration," a partnership with over 40 companies to analytically understand their sustainability challenges and provide practical solutions. Through the process, they found that "less than 5 percent of companies provide financial incentives or career opportunities for sustainability performance." This, senior experts Bonini and Swartz warn, creates an environment in which "people may not see the pursuit of sustainability as a way to build their career."[1]

To avoid this, you and your team can ensure that sustainability is the topic of one of the first conversations you have with new employees and that compliance becomes a key factor of their personal growth and success. Additionally, embedding sustainability education into team members' on-boarding (when newly hired), or during their yearly performance reviews, can help make an otherwise formal, and sometimes anxiety-producing process, more fun.

To further instill their commitment to the planet, New Resource Bank incorporates three phases of sustainability orientation into a new team member's first two weeks. The first is a brief, one-hour overview of all the institution's sustainability-related aspects.

The second session is a "Mission Training," which focuses on sharing the bank's mission, discussing the "old economy, the new economy, the real economy, and sustainability," says Meade. Third, new employees attend the "Green Team Training," which is a deeper dive into the bank's green initiatives, such as its waste diversion goals, Sustainability Engagement Program, and details about the Green Team activities.

Of course, the conversation doesn't stop with initiation. NRB's "Sustainability Engagement Program" is an internal educational program designed to advance all staff's sustainability knowledge. Spearheaded by the Green Team, the Sustainability Engagement Program serves as a way to quantify employees' engagement in the bank's sustainability initiatives and link their participation to their annual performance review.

To achieve a 5 out of 5 on the performance review, team members "have to earn 20 points within the Sustainable Engagement Program," Meade explains. "This is how we tangibly link sustainability to people's actual performance at the bank." Those points can be earned by attending the monthly sustainability-related Lunch & Learns, participating in webinars, or serving on the Green Team, the Best Places To Work Team (an affinity group that focuses on the bank's culture and employee happiness), or the Diversity & Inclusion Team. Employees can also earn points by reading a book or watching a movie that pertains to sustainability outside of work hours. The cumulative "sustainability score" contributes to 10% of each team member's overall score on the performance review.

The engagement program drives new members to the Green Team each year, all with fresh ideas to implement. "The program helps drive our culture of learning about sustainability," Meade shares. "It ensures knowledge building, demonstrates that it is a key part of our culture, and signals to employees how serious we take sustainability at our bank." This is an effective strategy to ensure that their lending decisions will have a long-term positive impact on the world.

Themes Support Deeper Understanding
Each year, NRB's Green Team selects a theme to direct the content of their activities. Whatever they select, they make sure to tie it back to their key lending goals: environmental protection, health and wellness, education and community empowerment, and sustainable commerce. In 2016, the annual theme was "Sustainable Fashion and Textiles," and "Health & Wellness" captured the spotlight in 2017. "We provide a lot of programming around our initiatives," says Meade. "Both in speakers we invite and documentaries we watch, as we take these as awareness and knowledge-building opportunities."

While the employees do not have a direct influence on the types of companies to which the bank lends, Meade shares that through NRB's educational programs and volunteer opportunities, employees become well-versed in matters of sustainability, and all team members gain a better understanding of the industries NRB serves. "Through the types of projects we fund, we fight climate change, support more sustainable food systems and better health, help schools expand, sustain the vital work of nonprofits in our communities and grow socially and environmentally responsible small businesses that are providing jobs with fair wages," she says.

A Fun Way to Learn
The "Sustainability Challenge" is another fun and educational program in which NRB encourages participation through annual review points. Each person chooses an area of sustainability that they are interested in learning more about and integrating into their lives. Examples include: growing your own garden at home, wasting less food, eating less meat, or decreasing automobile use through public transportation. The challenge is unique to each person and all projects turn out differently. This event creates yet another opportunity for people to learn more about sustainability and helps them transfer what they learn at the bank to their daily lives.

Each person earns three points for choosing a challenge and meets with a small team of people throughout the year to support one another in reaching their goals. These "mini-teams" meet quarterly to share progress and challenges, helping everyone stay on track. Last year, Meade's personal Sustainability Challenge was to grow food with her children—a goal that was shared by several other co-workers.

Another team member focused on eliminating palm oil from her diet. She called companies to ask about the source of the palm oil used in their products and shared her findings with all the team members. Learning about the positive and negative effects of this ubiquitous food source was a rewarding experience, one she maximized by sharing her newfound green wisdom with colleagues.

At the end of each year, everyone presents their Sustainability Challenge to the entire company. They make a party out of the gathering by enjoying food and laughter. It is a fun way to learn from each team member's passion, offer feedback, and pick up some new tips. "It's so inspiring to hear what people did all year, which gives ideas for the next year," says Meade. "People really go all out and get very involved with the research for their presentations." The Sustainability Challenge program is optional, but everyone, even those who aren't on the Green Team, has fun participating each year.

Supply Chain Education
Team members feel empowered when they become more aware and knowledgeable about the origin of company products. Understanding how raw materials become finished products creates a sense of personal ownership in the production process, building loyalty to the product and company alike. A more informed and involved workforce is a valuable asset to any company.

Alter Eco is dedicated to fair trade, organic practices and building ethical relationships with farmers. Company executives recognized that to achieve these commitments, they must first build a business culture that nurtures these values—starting with supply chain education. Almost all team members now travel to the countries where the food for Alter Eco products is sourced, an experience that causes Antoine Ambert, Director of Marketing at Alter Eco, to view the entire company as a Sustainability Team.

By visiting the farmers in Bolivia, Peru, Ecuador, Thailand, and India, team members get a better understanding of the farming cooperatives they work with and "really witness what we do here and the impact that we have, and how it impacts the lives of the farmers," Ambert explains. "It takes some time for the 22 people to travel so far, but it's worth it to uphold our mission." While not every company has the financial resources to execute this type of far-reaching educational program, Sustainability Teams in all companies can still learn about the exact origins of their products and share the information with other team members.

Dumpster Diving for Data

While it might sound unattractive, dumpster diving is a great way to provide an educational experience for all company team members. This event is far less glamorous than a Brown Bag Lunch, but it provides an opportunity for team members to get a first-hand look at the impact the company makes on the local landfill and can be a fun way to build a sense of team unity and involvement. Additionally, the data gathered can serve as the baseline for a waste audit, helping company leadership project important waste reduction goals. While it is serious business, leaders can turn dumpster dives into fun and educational events so everyone will get involved.

Polishing Transferable Skills

Taking a leadership position on a Sustainability Team requires and builds perseverance, courage, motivation, and passion. With every campaign, event, or initiative, Sustainability Team members cultivate skills that are assets in current and future positions and could help them move up the ladder in the future.

By participating in the work of a Sustainability Team, employees have an opportunity to use their abilities in a different context than their normal day-to-day responsibilities require. For example, in your company, you might have a team member in the Facilities Department who has zero training in marketing. However, as part of a Sustainability Team initiative, she might spearhead a rich and complex employee engagement program for the entire company. Without this opportunity, she and the company would have missed out on a valuable chance to grow.

Creating presentations, interfacing with contacts from different departments, coordinating initiatives with executives, and speaking in front of groups are all valuable ways for you, and everyone on the team, to grow transferable skills. Those who volunteer to lead a Sustainability Team (or even just participate in one!) will hone their leadership skills as they effectively execute campaigns that make a lasting impression throughout the organization.

To help your members grow their skills, ensure that your Sustainability Team provides employees with several of the following opportunities:

- **Organizational:** organize meetings, solve problems, plan and implement campaigns.

- **Interpersonal:** recruit new team members, resolve conflicts, build community relationships.

- **Managerial:** oversee budgets, create timelines, prioritize projects.

- **Communication:** write marketing or public relations plans, speak in front of audiences, listen to feedback.

- **Leadership:** share newfound sustainability knowledge, motivate a team, evaluate vendors.

- **Research & Analysis:** plan baselines for sustainability goals, measure campaign outcomes, develop metrics for future analysis.

Ojure finds it fulfilling to witness people establishing relationships and working on projects that never would have occurred without Earthforce. "Earthforce is such an incredible leadership and growth opportunity for people," she expresses. "We see individuals growing their skill sets and building incredible cross-functional relationships that can be used to grow their network."

Green Wisdom at Work and Home
Additionally, the Sustainability Team can provide information about how to "go green" at home, helping employees become more sustainable in their own day-to-day lives. This adds a personal touch to company initiatives and helps employees integrate the new practices even more deeply into their lives.

During a recent internal survey of Green Genes volunteers at Genentech, 87% of volunteers said they apply what they learn from Green Genes to their home life. The education and experience these volunteers attain at work through the Green Genes program has infused their lives outside of the office.

They authentically walk their talk, even outside Genentech's doors.

In a 2016 study conducted by Cone Communications, 83% of Millennials (those born in 1982 or after) surveyed said they want "their company to provide support and resources for them to make positive social and environmental changes at home."[2] Additionally, 89% of Millennials expect employers to provide hands-on activities that focus on environmental responsibilities in the workplace.[3] The next generation of the American workforce is motivated by making a meaningful difference—in their personal lives, and through the work of the company they support.

The Gifts of Participation
Being part of a Sustainability Team takes time and effort, but this is not without reward. Across industries, Sustainability Team members are gaining valuable new skills, finding enhanced purpose in their work, earning face time with company executives, and changing industry norms. Too often, environmental activism is reduced to guilt-tripping, but as these successful company initiatives show, Sustainability Teams are changing the stigma and building positive company cultures. When led by a shared vision and committed team members, Sustainability Teams are invaluable sources of corporate and personal growth that continues long after 5 o'clock.

The Earthforce Ohana Group

Salesforce's culture is built around the Hawaiian concept of Ohana, which means family. Ohana is the deep-seated support system inside the company that extends from its employees to its customers, partners and communities.

This value is embodied in its Ohana Groups. These are employee-led and employee-organized groups centered around common life experiences or backgrounds, and their allies.. In many other companies, these are called "affinity groups."

Salesforce has a framework which is used to set the annual work plans of each Ohana group, including Earthforce, one of the company's largest groups. This framework serves as each team's compass for the year, helping Earthforce and other Ohana groups craft their vision, set annual metrics, and promote collaboration and understanding among team members all over the world.

Earthforce also gets strategic support from the corporate Salesforce Sustainability Team. "This helps Earthforce better understand where the Sustainability

Team and the company are headed," says Ojure, Salesforce's Director of Sustainability. "Members can see how they fit into that big picture on both a regional and company-wide level."

The crossover has proved to be fun and effective, as it increases collaboration throughout the company. "One of the best things about working in sustainability is the opportunity to collaborate with so many folks around the organization and get a comprehensive view of the business," says Ojure.

Notes

1. Sheila Bonini and Steven Swartz, "Profits with Purpose: How Organizing for Sustainability Can Benefit the Bottom Line," McKinsey & Company (July 2014), p. 5, https://www.mckinsey.com/~/media/McKinsey/Business%20Functions/Sustainability%20and%20Resource%20Productivity/Our%20Insights/Profits%20with%20purpose/Profits%20with%20Purpose.ashx (Accessed October 8, 2018).
2. "2016 Cone Communications Millennial Employee Engagement Study," Cone Communications (April 2016), p. 7, https://static1.squarespace.com/static/56b4a7472b8dde3df5b7013f/t/5819e8b303596e3016ca0d9c/1478092981243/2016+Cone+Communications+Millennial+Employee+Engagement+Study_Press+Release+and+Fact+Sheet.pdf (Accessed October 8, 2018).
3. Ibid, p. 2.

8

Your Fun Campaigns Can Bring Results

Making Sustainability Memorable
Decreasing your company's environmental footprint and developing campaigns that create climate change awareness is serious and important work. As your team members become immersed in it, perhaps for the first time, it's possible that some might become mired in the doom and gloom of our planet's environmental challenges. It is important that leaders balance the seriousness of the current problem with an optimistic outlook on the positive impact the team is making. Volunteers want to dedicate their time to a

worthy cause, but remember, they are giving up their free time for this—volunteer work should also be fun and energizing.

One goal of your Sustainability Team is to create enjoyable, engaging, and educational events that people will be excited to attend and remember into the future. Fun experiences affect minds and hearts and keep team and community members coming back for more. If the team comes across as boring or "too corporate," people will stop attending meetings, and the team's momentum will fizzle out.

Incorporating enjoyable team-bonding activities into your Sustainability Team meetings is a great strategy to form deeper connections among team members. At Dr. Bronner's, before the start of a Green Team meeting everyone shares "two truths about their lives." It's an easy and free way to decrease any stress people might feel about their regular responsibilities and prepare them for a sustainability brainstorming session.

The interpersonal connections that make up the team are assets that are both important and challenging to quantify. Like the Operations or Marketing departments, the Sustainability Team works best when members possess a baseline of trust, strong communication skills, and high rates of collaboration. Sustainability Teams can fine-tune these skills and characteristics through memorable experiences that create a sense of community. If it's not fun to be on a Sustainability Team, people will not participate!

Here are some simple activities to bring more fun into your Sustainability Team meetings:

- **Quiz Time:** at the beginning of each meeting, start with a short quiz to test the team's knowledge of the month's sustainability theme. Possible themes are endless!

- **Movie Lunch:** host a movie lunch and show a film in two increments over two weeks (since most people take an hour for lunch). Leave 20 minutes for discussion during the second gathering so attendees can hear each other's perspectives. There are many informative documentaries on topics such as sustainable food, conscious investing, animal protection, plastic reduction, and more.

- **Share Your Passions:** start each meeting by learning about everyone's "passion as it relates to sustainability." People often engage in strategies at home that help to decrease waste, conserve the earth's resources, and save money. Sharing this homegrown green wisdom with colleagues creates a ripple effect of information that will soon have a big impact.

- **Play Games:** oversee interoffice competitions. The Sustainability Team can devise fun ways for people in all departments to participate in a shared experience. For example, a "Rideshare Challenge." The goal of this campaign is to increase carpooling and decrease gasoline use over a specific period. The Sustainability Team can compile this information and measure the impact of each department's actions. The Sustainability Team will need to adjust calculations for the total distance and number of team members in each department.

Climate change is getting more serious every day, and the relevant business concerns are sobering. However, as the University of Oxford and Arabesque Partners conclude, "Properly implemented, superior sustainability policies can mitigate aspects of [climate] risks by prompting pre-emptive action."[1] Theory and data are helpful, but as these featured companies demonstrate, producing campaigns that appeal to Sustainability Team members, as well as employees who are not aware of the company's earth-focused initiatives, is key to inspiring the pre-emptive action the world so desperately needs. By approaching this sensitive issue with lighthearted fun, you can maximize engagement and impact.

Eliminating Vampire Power
Being silly (with a purpose) is an excellent way for you and your colleagues to maintain an optimistic outlook on the pressing issue of climate change, while also contributing to climate solutions. Creating programs, events, and initiatives that facilitate learning and implementing new conservation steps, while at the same time encouraging team members if they make mistakes, is an important balance for all teams.

At Genentech, a small sub-team within the Energy Committee is lovingly called "The Army of Darkness." This grim-sounding, yet very effective group saves energy by turning off lights, monitors, and other appliances when people have forgotten, thereby decreasing or eliminating "vampire power." Vampire power occurs when equipment is turned off, yet still plugged into an electrical outlet, slowly but continuously draining a small bit of energy. Every small bit of vampire energy adds up, and decreasing it saves money!

Employees from all Genentech offices volunteer for this subcommittee, which organizes itself online and boasts its own logo: a little cell phone with bat wings and vampire fangs. When Genentech moved, The Army of Darkness was responsible for ensuring that motion detectors and smart lighting systems were integrated into the new buildings. As Green Genes director Katie Excoffier notes, "They are really the boots on the ground to let the energy manager know what is working and areas to do even better"

The Army's work demonstrates that participating on the Green Genes team does not always need to be a major time commitment. As you develop your own sustainability programs, follow Excoffier's suggestion and "try to get employees involved in fun ways and make them feel like they can make a difference."

No Preaching Allowed
Environmental activism can bear a stigma of negativity, but, with a bit of creativity, your Sustainability Team can make employee engagement programs a lot of fun. Building a fun and inclusive culture around the work of the Sustainability Team will go further towards recruiting new partners than the most convincing logical argument.

The Sustainability Team at Badger used a social marketing strategy that integrated its community activities to improve employee's awareness of their plastic use. Members posted a sign that said, "I pledge to do my best not to use plastic for one week, and any plastic I do use will be placed in the 'Dilemma Bin.'" The sign and bin were placed in the lunchroom for everyone to see, and one-third of the company signed the pledge to participate.

Sustainability Committee leaders did not check on the employees or ask them how their "plastic-free pledge" was going. They didn't need to, because they found that the participants voluntarily shared their successes and challenges. In turn, Sustainability Manager Jess Baum would respond with a story about an aspect in her life where she felt conflicted about a sustainability decision to demonstrate that she's not perfect either, but she's trying! "We're cautious to walk that line between education, engagement, and preaching," she shares. "We don't want to alienate or judge anyone." Throughout the process, leaders shared how they practiced sustainability in their own lives to lead by example. Badger's Collaborative Executive Officer Rebecca Hamilton adds, "there's constantly a lot going on throughout people's lives and we need to respect that, while also trying to inspire and educate."

One particular team member loved the plastic-free challenge so much that she became one of the champions for Badger's waste auditing practices. She also took it upon herself to collect a list of zero-waste blogs to share with everyone and even began using reusable bamboo utensils and a glass straw when eating away from home. These are small actions that add up over time and are prime examples of the personal impact fun corporate sustainability initiatives can have on everyone involved.

Lunch Mapping
Whether growing, shopping, cooking, or eating, people love to relate with one another through food. To help employees learn about the environmental impact of the foods they eat, the Sustainability Committee at Badger hosted a lunch that showed "how far your food traveled."

They placed different food items from their lunch in proportional distance from a "home" base. The Zoli tuna fish from Thailand was placed far in the back, while the food items from their local areas of New Hampshire were much closer and items from California landed in between. Each item had a sign that reported the name of the location and the number of miles traveled. Committee members stood at each food item and shared why the Badger chefs decided to source the food for lunch from these specific areas. For example, while the tuna traveled 8,000 miles, the leaders knew that it was caught wild and sustainably. Had the fish been procured from closer distances, it would have been caught in nets or other unsustainable ways. This type of engaging, hands-on activity can be replicated in any company cafeteria or lunchroom.

Rebecca Hamilton, a Badger family member, understands the need for a connection between team members' and the company's goals. "I think the value and benefit of the Sustainability Committee is that it inspires individuals to have a greater appreciation for what sustainability means and what our mission means," she says. "Then, as employees are making each decision for their job, where they have ownership responsibility and a larger impact in the company, they have this sensibility in part from the inspiration that comes from the sustainability committee."

Rewards for Commuting
Organizing a commuting or rideshare program can have a multifaceted impact. Ridesharing decreases the amount of pollution in the air, the space needed for parking lots, and employee stress. In the ultimate win-win-win scenario, these programs have proven to be beneficial for the company, the team members, and the earth!

The Green Genes Transportation team leaders work with gRide, Genentech's rideshare program, to help promote greener commute options. Green Genes, gRide, and Genentech's Bike Club co-sponsor "Bike To Work Day" during "Transportation Month" each May, offering people the opportunity to test drive electric bikes and electric vehicles throughout the month.

By participating in the rideshare program, employees can save money on fuel and tolls, in addition to helping the environment by decreasing CO_2 emissions. Since fewer parking spots are needed, Genentech has more campus green spaces. "We calculate our CO_2 emissions every year from the commute program, and our emissions per employee are trending downward," says Excoffier.

In 2014, Genentech celebrated the 100,000,000[th] mile traveled in a Genentech bus to or from work. To celebrate this sustainability win, Green Genes and gRide co-hosted a large "Eco Fair." Thanks to 100 Green Genes volunteers, the event was a huge success. Everyone had a lot of fun, especially those who pedaled stationary bikes to power blenders, the sound system, and spin art machines.

To top it off, four courageous Green Genes members climbed onto the stage—in front of 2,000 people in a big conference center—and sang Green Genes-modified versions of rock classics, with words changed to share about energy efficiency. Karaoke screens were installed so others could join in on the fun.

Zero Waste Zones
Moving offices can create a lot of waste. Furniture, electronics, and office supplies are replaced or discarded and can end up in landfills. With a strategic plan, many of these items can be reused or donated, and new owners can put it all to good use.

In 2016, Genentech opened a new building with an open floor plan. Instead of a cubicle (complete with shelves and drawers), employees now had a desk with just one drawer in an open-floored office. On average, each team member had eleven boxes of papers and office supplies to move, yet their new office space did not have the capacity for so much "stuff" per person.

The Sustainability Team knew they needed to take drastic action to mitigate the landfill waste that could result from this big move. So, before each department of the company took its turn to move buildings, the team created "Zero Waste Zones" in every area. These zones had boxes for different office materials, such as binders, books, decorations, and other supplies. People sorted all of the items they didn't need into the boxes. Before moving, other employees could come through and shop for anything they needed. Afterward, the items (including 2,000 computer monitors) were donated to local schools. "It had a really big impact on our waste and on the visibility of our program," Excoffier recalls, "because everyone got to participate and make an impact not to just recycle and throw things away, but to reuse items."

The program was so successful Genentech decided to utilize Zero Waste Zones for all remodels and moves, from small to large. The zones received a branded look and are kept clean through collaboration with the warehouse operations team which picks up the items for donation when the boxes are full.

Brainstorming Sessions Provide Inspiration
A productive brainstorming session, where everyone freely shares their ideas and perspectives, can be a fun and revitalizing way for you to inspire laughter and connection. Planning a productive brainstorming session might take some work, but the creativity that takes place can be the catalyst for change.

As explored in Chapter 7, New Resource Bank strategically educates their team about sustainability topics while at the same time creating a fun and supportive atmosphere for everyone. At the beginning of each year, the Green Team gathers twice to brainstorm ideas for the coming year. "Everybody takes two minutes and writes down every single idea for what the Green Team could accomplish in the next year, no matter how crazy," Meade shares. This exercise helps team members build relationships around their shared interests.

Having Fun in the Trash
Company dumpster dives can be the centerpiece of a full or half-day event that brings people from all departments together to have fun, create memories, and educate everyone involved about the amount of waste going into the landfill (while also inspiring conversations and ideas that will help improve that number).

Analyzing energy use can feel vague to people who learn by doing. A dumpster dive is a practical, hands-on way for people to understand a critical company process. Genentech's Green Genes organizes periodic dumpster dives as a way to integrate fun and education. This is one of the things that employees can see and easily get involved in.

Both the dumpster dives and Zero Waste Zones (in addition to other landfill reduction initiatives) have made a significant impact on Genentech's waste reduction goals. Since 2010, the company has reduced its waste by 55% and is on track to achieve its goal of 80% reduction per employee. The Green Genes volunteers have been instrumental in supporting the company as it becomes more sustainable and develops a lighter footprint. Since its inception, Green Genes has helped the company divert over 360,000 pounds from the landfill and save approximately $20,000 in landfill fees.

You might assume that dumpster diving attracts only the most dedicated employees, but in reality, dumpster dive days at Dr. Bronner's always bring a large number of people from all departments. The Green Team creates a fun environment to make the gathering one of the most-attended events of the year. "Volunteer Dumpster Divers get to wear limited edition, really cool branded swag, we have great food and great music playing all day, and it's a really fun day," says Shiber-Knowles. Regardless of the industry, every company has trash. Dumpster dives offer a great way for your Sustainability Team to combine important research with employee engagement.

Helpful Angels Sharing Green Wisdom
Paper waste, food waste, increased water or energy use, and air travel all make an impact on the environment when your company hosts a conference, workshop, or fair. It is now expected that companies develop programs to mitigate event impact and assemble teams to ensure that the programs are completed. With executive support and creativity, these events offer Sustainability Teams a platform to demonstrate that even your company's largest functions can be climate-friendly and educational.

Corporate events are ready-made opportunities for the team to bring sustainability to life and connect with customers in a new way. Salesforce's annual conference, Dreamforce, has become one of the most fun and impactful times of the year for the Earthforce team. While the conference is not focused on sustainability, the Earthforce team has found that this is a perfect opportunity for its volunteers to share their knowledge and engage the more than 170,000 conference attendees from around the world.

To reduce waste-to-landfill, the Earthforce team carries out a comprehensive, yet simple program called the "Green Angel Program." During the event, employee volunteers (Green Angels) stand next to the bins and show attendees how to sort their waste (compost, recycling, landfill). Conference attendees are very receptive to the direction which creates a fun learning opportunity about waste processes—especially compost. "Many people don't have composting at home," Ojure shares. "They look at our compostable lunch box and they have no idea what to do, so our volunteers help them sort everything from their meal. It seems like such a simple moment but many volunteers tell me that talking with customers about sustainability was their favorite moment of the week."

We've all stood in front of those bins and questioned where to put each item. At a massive conference like Dreamforce, any decrease in waste output is important. "Dreamforce is an incredible time for us to engage our larger community, use our voice, and show off our passion," says Ojure. "It's just a beautiful example, and a reminder to me, that the initiatives don't have to be big and flashy—they can be very simple and still be effective."

To Your Health
Personal health and wellness is important for everyone. Sustainability Teams can support all members of the company by creating entertaining ways to keep the mind and body healthy.

Malkin-Weber shares that members of the Environmental Stewardship Committee at Self-Help Credit Union participate in a meditation challenge, stair-climbing challenge, or both. Desired milestones and goals for each challenge are shared with other team members, and everyone reports their weekly progress. These challenges are a fun way to encourage others and stay motivated.

In addition to spearheading a "running challenge," where employees supported a non-profit client by forming small teams to raise money for the most collective miles, the Green Team at New Resource Bank was inspired to take action on the many conversations they were having about water issues in California. When they discovered that 1,825 gallons of water are used to produce only one pound of beef (compared to 39 gallons of water to produce a pound of vegetables), Green Team members realized that they could make a difference by implementing a "Meatless Monday" initiative. Other co-workers agreed because the new initiative enjoyed a 65% participation rate.

Every Monday, a Green Team member sends out vegetarian recipes to help people stay motivated, creating fun conversations between people during lunch. "I think it raised awareness of how much meat people consume and the importance of eating less meat for a healthier planet," Meade explains. "It establishes a sense of community of all doing something together, which is great. Also, I learned an awesome new recipe for roasted carrots and lentils that I cook all the time now!"

As Fun as Impactful
Since Sustainability Teams are usually volunteer-led, activities need to be as fun as they are impactful to a company's bottom line. This combination will help

you ensure that people continue to participate and the company continues to support the team's endeavors. Whether you're eating burritos around a dumpster, sharing lentil recipes, or cramming your co-workers into a borrowed mini-van, emphasize fun and creativity. You're doing more than making sustainability entertaining; you're building an engaging culture that will change the way you do business and brighten up your workplace—even as you're turning out the lights!

The Big Picture: A Year-Long Sustainability Road Map Everyone Can Use

The chapter 6 pullout outlined how your Sustainability Team can develop engaging community events by strategically selecting a format, location, community partners, and fun activities that support the team's goals. This chapter shares how the Sustainability Committee at Badger Balm has taken this kind of strategic thinking to the next level—developing a multi-tiered sustainability campaign in which each event and initiative builds upon the last.

To pursue further alignment between company values and the actual impact of their supply chain, the leadership team at Badger chose to make "Sustainable Sourcing" the focus of a yearlong theme. In support of this effort, the Sustainability Committee created four different weeks of sustainability-focused events throughout the year to mobilize and empower their co-workers. Employees participated by watching films, enjoying events, and taking part in activities that allowed them to learn more about sustainable sourcing and make impactful changes in their own lives and the life of the company.

Rather than offering a random assortment of events, the Sustainability Committee chose a format that strategically increased engagement throughout the year. Building from Awareness Week to Connection Week, Commitment Week, and finally, Ongoing Action Week, the committee was able to build long-term momentum.

The following is an outline of the events that Badger Balm used to fully integrate their sustainability themes into the company's day-to-day operations. Theme weeks were held throughout the year:

Awareness Week: (the week leading up to Earth Day)
The goal of "Awareness Week" is to educate employees about the impacts of their purchasing, both at work and in their homes. The Sustainability Committee designed visually stimulating signage that displayed supply chain maps of commonly purchased items or explained the hidden costs of paying less. In addition to a company meeting that focused on Badger's ingredient sourcing, other activities included:

- **Newsletter** - the committee distributed a special edition of the company newsletter, "What's Up Badger," featuring employee stories about sustainable sourcing in their personal lives.

- **Short videos** - employees enjoyed educational videos during breaks, including

The Story of Stuff, Surfing for Change, and a short video about a woman who created only a quart of trash in one year.

- **Lunch Mapping** - this interactive activity explored the question, "How far does your food travel?" (described above).

Connection Week
The goal of Connection Week is to encourage dialogue and the sharing of experiences, tips, and ideas among employees. The Sustainability Committee also engaged with other businesses to share big-picture opportunities for positive change.

- **Local Lunch** - joined by special guests involved with the local food system, everyone enjoyed a delicious lunch featuring all local ingredients.

- **Clothes Swap** - people brought their old clothes and traded them for clothes brought by others (otherwise known as "new-to-me." Clothes not selected were donated to a local not-for-profit organization).

- **Needs and Offers** - the committee offered a special section of the "What's Up Badger" newsletter featuring ads for people to buy, sell, or barter goods that might otherwise become waste.

Commitment Week
The goal of Commitment Week is to engage employees in positive actions that encourage commitment to the company's sustainable values at work and home.

- **Plastic Free Challenge** - Badger asked team members to pledge to use no plastic, or even just less plastic. "By offering a challenge-by-choice opportunity for employees to make meaningful change in a supportive environment, we were able to engage without preaching to those who chose not to participate," says Baum. "Through building the challenge around acceptance that no one is perfect (having the dilemma bin), we invited more widespread and authentic participation."

- **Abundance Table** - employees brought items they wanted to share with others, such as produce from their own gardens, and baked or canned goods.

- **Badger Bulk Buying Program** - a new experiment, this group purchasing program allowed employees to use collective buying power to save money on bulk amounts of organic rice, beans, and popcorn.

Ongoing Action Week
During this week, the Sustainability Committee hosted events that recognized the employees' successes in making sustainable choices in their personal and professional lives.

- **Tire Pressure Check** - according to the Department of Energy, "Under-inflated tires can lower gas mileage by about 0.2% for every 1 psi drop in the average pressure of all tires."[2] Since many people at Badger commute up to 25 miles round trip, those percentage points add up in a hurry. An inflation station was set up in the parking lot so drivers could maximize their car's efficiency.

- **Winter Local Lunch** - this lunch featured delicious, locally grown food, showcasing the abundance of healthy produce available year round. Baum notes, "winters in northern New England don't bring to mind an abundance of locally-cultivated food. Our winter local lunch brought awareness to the local bounty that exists even in the dead of winter and shed light on ways we could look to rely on local food more throughout all four seasons."

- **Junk Mail Round-Up** - "We had actually noticed that we were receiving the same catalogs many times!" says Baum. "As a result, we collected all junk mail with the goal of no longer getting any catalogs we didn't need or want." Instead of ten people calling separately to get themselves off the same mailing list, one person took on the responsibility for everyone, saving the others precious time (perhaps giving them a chance to call other catalog companies if needed).

This simple framework is a powerful guide for supporting your company's climate change initiatives.

Adapt yearly and weekly themes to your company culture, values, and employee's level of sustainability-related knowledge, and you have a formula for years of sustainability success.

Notes

1. Gordon L. Clark, Andreas Feiner, and Michael Viehs, "From the Stockholder to the Stakeholder: How Sustainability Can Drive Financial Outperformance," Arabesque Partners and University of Oxford (March 2015), p. 16, https://arabesque.com/research/From_the_stockholder_to_the_stakeholder_web.pdf (Accessed October 8, 2018).
2. "Keeping Your Vehicle in Shape," U.S. Department of Energy (June 27, 2016), https://www.fueleconomy.gov/feg/maintain.jsp (Accessed October 8, 2018).

9

Inspiring Your Company to "Walk the Talk"

Everyone Can Walk the Talk
"Walking the talk" means ensuring that day-to-day actions reflect the values a person or company promotes. For example, if your website states that your company has the environment in mind with every action it takes, yet in practice, dumps hazardous waste into local waterways, your company is not walking the talk. However, if your company shares that it commits to the environment, and that commitment leads you or another team member to

organize a river cleanup day with company employees, your company *is* walking the talk.

While corporations are not people, they are made of people. The Sustainability Teams at the companies interviewed are composed of caring, knowledgeable employees who walk their talk by volunteering their time and giving back to their communities and the planet. Inside and outside of their offices, these individuals are building genuinely sustainable businesses whose actions are in alignment with their overall vision and values.

Your company can't walk its talk unless all team members and executives closely analyze their communications, supply chain, operational processes, and more. When your CEO and executives incorporate sustainability into their decision-making process, other employees are inspired, and conscious consumers take notice.

Connecting Sustainability Efforts to Worklife
Promoting awareness and education within its workforce is a crucial part of any company's commitment to environmental care. The best practices and tips employees learn at work go home with them at the end of the day, magnifying the company's positive environmental impact.

During a recent survey of Green Genes volunteers at Genentech, 99% of respondents shared that it is important for them to work at a company that is environmentally responsible. When asked, "What have you learned from participating in Green Genes that you have been able to apply to your job at work?" 87% of the respondents said that they could apply tips that they've learned through their participation with Green Genes to their jobs. "I just love that statistic!" Excoffier exclaims. Many of the hands-on activities that volunteers take on build valuable, transferable skills and experience.

The survey results showed that by volunteering in the Green Genes program, employees learned new information and also helped the company save resources and money. That is quite a business case for sustainability!

Drought to Development
New Resource Bank and Genentech found that reducing corporate and individual water usage can be a great way to start walking the talk.

"In 2014, our team brainstormed and decided to make an impact on the planet by focusing on the drought," shares Meade of NRB. Since the bank leases an office in a large building in downtown San Francisco that is already LEED Gold certified, they didn't need to upgrade building infrastructure. As they considered their options, Meade and the team realized that the best way they could personally reduce their water usage was by reducing their meat consumption since the meat industry is such a large consumer of water.

While this might sound like a small step, their water reduction efforts made an impact (as mentioned in Chapter 8). Approximately 65% of the bank's employees pledged to consume a plant-based diet each Monday for a full year. According to Support Meat Free Monday, 888 gallons of water are saved when one person skips eating meat one day a week for a year.[1] Thanks to the 26 NRB employees who participated in Meatless Monday, this fun campaign saved over 23,000 gallons of water in a single year!

Genentech's Green Genes members were also worried about the recent drought in California. In fact, in 2015 water conservation topped the list of issues members thought the group should focus on. Genentech dove into the campaign, knowing that raising awareness and developing new programs that use less water at work would change employee behavior at home too—making an even more significant impact. "When we let our lawns 'go gold' on campus, and then explain to employees why this is important, they are more likely to reduce how much they water their own lawns," Excoffier says.

Integrating sustainable behavior into personal life is a focus of many of Green Genes' monthly themes. Lunch and Learn topics have included everything from information on solar panels to how to raise chickens or bees. The company has also given away recycled barrels so employees could collect rain for their gardens! These are all ways that Sustainability Teams can walk their talk and use their efforts to influence the habits and patterns of everyone in the company—even while they are at home!

Focusing on Waste
Many of the companies interviewed for this book walk their talk by striving to get closer to overall zero waste. Each year, they calibrate their operations to find better ways to reuse or recycle so their waste output number decreases. For well-established companies, drastic changes can be challenging and unnerving. Thankfully huge improvements can be

achieved in small steps when everyone on the team works together.

A suggestion about workspace layout made by a Green Team volunteer who works in the shipping department at Dr. Bronner's made a huge impact on decreasing waste output in 2017 (see the pullout at the end of the chapter for more). By merely changing the manner in which they collect and process waste, the company was able to see a significant drop in waste output, even while production increased. "That's a win that we've been able to see in the last year," Shiber-Knowles reflects.

While the Green Team at Dr. Bronner's will analyze and reduce the company's waste output first, the team is excited to tackle many different aspects of sustainability that will motivate a bigger cross-section of the entire company over time. "I anticipate that we will touch all aspects of our environmental footprint and potential handprint over the coming years," Shiber-Knowles shares. "We have a solid foundation for tackling our waste goals first, and I imagine we'll next look at water use and electricity, start an on-site composting process, and we'll probably do some cool water and grey water projects."

Shiber-Knowles says that the team members at Dr. Bronner's have also talked about researching more effective construction and demolition practices and installing hand dryers in all bathrooms, in addition to focusing on their social and environmental purchasing policy. With so many potential areas to contribute, she believes that even more team members will be excited about contributing their energy and green wisdom into at least one project.

Mountain Rose Herbs is another business that is walking their talk and taking responsibility for their actions through their waste reduction initiatives, all of which have been greatly influenced and inspired by the efforts of their Green Team members.

In 2015, MRH diverted 96.2% of its waste. This means that only 3.8% of all material that left the company's site went to landfill. As a result, MRH became the first TRUE Zero Waste Certified company in Oregon by Green Business Certification Inc. The title is a big victory for the company and a motivating factor to continue striving towards 100% waste diversion. While this feat required buy-in from all levels of the company, Bascue attributes the Zero Waste award to the Green Team and facilities staff. "Our facilities crew members are really the ones who made this happen," she says. "They sort every piece of material that's put in the trash bin and all the different bins. They examine the material and decide whether it can be upcycled or recycled. Without our devoted staff, we couldn't have achieved this goal."

For MRH, packing peanuts represent one of the challenges embedded in that last 4%. Dry herbs sourced from vendors in the Pacific Northwest arrive at their facility with minimal packing waste. However, despite requesting that their vendors stop using packing peanuts, the fragile items that MRH sells, such as teapots and tincture containers, continue to arrive at their headquarters surrounded by the small, puffy, pieces of styrofoam.

The company could simply externalize the issue, passing along the peanuts to those who purchase the fragile items, but Bascue knows that MRH customers would not appreciate opening a package awash in tiny little pieces of styrofoam—even if MRH is reusing the material.

To ensure that the little peanuts do not end up in a landfill, a Green Team member from the receiving department formulated a simple solution. MRH formed relationships with local non-profit organizations that can use or recycle the styrofoam peanuts. A point person in the Receiving Department collects, sorts, and stores the peanuts in large bags before transporting them to the new location. "It is challenging to find a partner who will consistently take the volume [of styrofoam peanuts] that we have," admits Bascue.

While it would be easier to put the peanuts into the dumpster once the boxes of breakable teapots from other parts of the world are opened, Mountain Rose Herbs walks its talk by dedicating time and energy into finding a way to recycle or reuse these small plastic bits.

Analyzing and fine-tuning waste processes is one of the many ways the Green Team members work together on issues that have a direct impact on the entire company. Though their work was not motivated by winning prestigious awards, being named the first TRUE Zero Waste company in the state sure doesn't hurt!

Optimizing to Save Resources
The efforts of your company's Sustainability Team are especially valuable when the company itself does not have the resources needed to effectively monitor and evaluate the environmental impact of its own

processes. Knowledgeable individuals on the Sustainability Team can use their skills to analyze the functionality of machinery, procure environmentally-friendly supplies, and even work with local and federal agencies to secure rebates on energy-saving equipment.

The Sustainability Council at Better World Books (BWB) continually optimizes their operations to ensure that the company walks its talk. The company measures and evaluates data and performance through the use of Key Performance Indicators (data the company values as the most important metrics for measuring sustainability initiatives), environmental impact metrics, third-party assessments, certifications, annual carbon audits, and overall company objectives. Regularly reviewing company financial statements is also an important practice that helps executives see how the Sustainability Council is supporting the company's sustainability goals.

This commitment to operational analysis brought the Sustainability Council's attention to their packaging process. Each package of books that BWB ships to customers contains a packing slip, a piece of paper that details the shipment particulars and the buyer's contact information.

That piece of paper may seem like a small matter, but the Council knows that small changes make significant impacts. BWB wants to "make sure that we're not shipping more packaging around the world than what we need to," says Holland. When working with the quantities BWB ships, "it adds up," he confirms. "One of the biggest things we see in our carbon/garbage audit every year is the impact of this activity."

Over the course of a year, millions of these sheets are generated, but BWB's Sustainability Council aims to eliminate this waste and re-engineer the process. This represents a significant challenge, but also a tremendous opportunity. Making the shift to more innovative packaging technology, while also decreasing unnecessary paper use, will help the company save over $250,000 a year. As a result, BWB will see the return on this sustainability-related investment in less than a year.

Though upgrading from the current homegrown system to a larger enterprise software system is a significant IT and Operations task, the move will mean increased alignment between the company's values and actions. The significant savings in printer and cartridge costs doesn't hurt either. "Especially in our business where every penny counts," adds Holland.

The Importance of the Supply Chain
What takes place along your company's supply chain is just as important as what happens in the main office or company headquarters. According to a 2010 Business For Social Responsibility & United Nations Global Compact study on "Supply Chain Sustainability," companies are seen to be "responsible" when their vendors comply with environmental regulations, management treats their employees well, and the products and services are designed to use the least amount of resources possible.[2] A sustainable and responsible company is in alignment with its values when it takes the time to

collaborate with its vendors and ensure that its entire supply chain is sustainable.

Alter Eco is 100% fair trade, and "sustainability is really the DNA" of the company, shares Director of Marketing Antoine Ambert. The company pays fair trade prices to their farming cooperative partners in Peru, Ecuador, India, and other countries that supply it with the necessary products needed to produce their food. Their dedication to all the contributing members of their supply chain has a ripple effect: the farmers sell their crops to the cooperative at a fair price, which means that despite market price fluctuations, the farmers are paid a living wage so that they can feed their families and send their children to school.

Alter Eco then purchases the products from the farming cooperatives (again, at a fair trade price). In addition, a Fair Trade Premium is paid to the cooperative farming members to fund community development programs that increase educational possibilities for local students, provide health and vision analysis for community members, add to infrastructure improvement for the community buildings, offer interest-free loans for businesses, and fund reforestation projects that help with long-term agricultural projects. "Everything we do revolves around sustainability and we take into consideration the impact that every point on the supply chain has on every stakeholder—from the farmers to the environment," says Ambert.

Supplies from the Sea
Further demonstrating their commitment to a sustainable supply chain, as a result of Interface's

Mission Zero, company researchers have been assessing and optimizing the life cycle impact of all of the materials used to make its products.

Nylon, a material composed of petroleum-based plastic that has an incredibly high environmental footprint, is one of the primary components of carpet making. For Interface to achieve "zero footprint," the company needed to reassess its entire carpet-making process. "Unless we found a way to use low-impact nylon, we would never have a sustainable product and achieve zero footprint," says Davis. In a real demonstration of green wisdom, Interface realized that to reach its goal, all of its suppliers would also need to go on the sustainability journey with them.

Interface developed a new business relationship with Aquafil, an Italian company that was happy to be part of Interface's future goals and developments. By innovating its technology, Aquafil now produces 100% recycled nylon, dramatically decreasing the footprint for both businesses.

As a result, Interface has been able to introduce some "higher pile" (shaggier) carpets into their product line without increasing their use of plastics from new petroleum.

"If you put more virgin nylon on a carpet tile, the footprint goes through the roof," Davis explains. "Now we're willing to make some shaggier carpet because it doesn't have the huge footprint normally associated with using that much nylon in a product."

Again, the ripple effects continued beyond Interface, or even Aquafil, to other far-off destinations. In addition to recycling old carpet to make new carpet yarn, Interface's Net-Works initiative provides Aquafil with nylon material from fishing villages in the Philippines and Africa, and in doing so provides an alternative to throwing used fishing nets into landfills or back out into the sea. This new process benefits these communities by turning a waste product into an income source.

For Interface, the next step on their sustainability journey is moving beyond Mission Zero and into Climate Take Back. This initiative involves Interface creating products with materials that contain atmospheric carbon so that every product they make is a net carbon sink and therefore part of the climate solution. Announced in 2017, Interface's Proof Positive Tile is a prototype carpet tile that has a net negative carbon footprint, meaning that from raw material extraction to final manufacturing, each square meter of this carpet tile would remove two kilograms of CO_2 from the atmosphere.

Successes like these don't go unnoticed. Owens-Corning, a worldwide company that produces insulation, roofing, and fiberglass composites is five times larger than Interface and supplies the company with a small fiberglass cloth that fits in the middle of the carpet tiles. "We're a small customer, but we had a huge impact on them," says Davis.

Following Interface's sustainability lead, Owens Corning developed net positive goals for their operations and invested in windmills and solar arrays to power their manufacturing site in Ohio. Other companies, such as Nike and Walmart (neither of which are even in Interface's supply chain), have looked to Interface to help devise their zero footprint goals. Large, multinational companies are looking to Interface for leadership as they walk the talk and invite other businesses to join them. It's all part of what Interface's Climate Take Back framework calls, "Leading an Industrial Re-revolution."

The Green Wisdom Ripple Effect
Walking the talk isn't easy. Sometimes it means overhauling decades-old operational systems or tracing sustainability issues down the supply chain and asking people on the other side of the world to change their behavior. But as these examples show, your relentless commitment to positive action, even within a small group, can transform the way a whole industry does business. Whether it starts at the top or the bottom, awareness and care at any level changes how people relate to their roles and can lead to solutions that reach far beyond the company doors.

A Cross-Departmental Team in Practice

In 2017 Josh Alvarado, a team member from the Shipping Department at Dr. Bronner's, came to Shiber-Knowles with an idea. He had participated in a recent dumpster dive which got him thinking about the ways he could contribute to the company's sustainability efforts, especially within his department.

Alvarado noticed that team members' movements around the warehouse could be more efficient as they sorted recycling and waste. "I saw that so many of the items from the dumpster dive bins were from the Shipping Department that weren't getting recycled, but thrown away," he says. The Shipping Department was broken down into four teams, each with three members. Rather than sorting materials into the recycling bins, everyone threw items into whatever trash bins were closest to them.

Alvarado proposed that the (very large) sorting bins in the warehouse be organized in the same manner as the bins used to sort during a yearly dumpster dive. Shiber-Knowles organized a meeting with a few representatives and managers from the Shipping Department to get approval for this pilot project.

The Shipping Department became the first department to choose how it sorts recycling and waste on a departmental level, serving as a role model for other business units. Alvarado, who has his eyes on how things *really* work in his position and his department, made an important contribution to the company's waste sorting process—a contribution made possible by his being a part of the company's Green Team.

The results are fantastic. Lessons learned in the Shipping sorting pilot directly informed the design of the comprehensive, company-wide waste sorting program. In 2017 the company became revenue positive with their waste stream and went from paying a landfill company to take their waste away to "being paid for the materials we can upcycle, reuse, recycle, and divert," says Shiber-Knowles. With the money earned from recycling their waste and saving money on landfill costs, the company purchased a baler, which is used to organize and pack the recycled material. That upgrade will, in turn, increase the revenue for the base material.

From Josh's perspective, "It's helpful to have Green Team members from every department involved so they have an eye on everything going on in their respective departments. It would be strange for people to make rules in areas that don't have anything to do with them," he points out. "Ideas really start to flow during our Green Team meetings!"

Thanks to Alvarado's input, the Shipping Department has become instrumental in supporting the company's goal of reaching zero waste.

Notes

1. Support Meat Free Mondays, "Facts and Figures," Fry's Vegetarian (2012) http://www.supportmfm.co.za/ (Accessed October 8, 2018).
2. Cody Sisco, Blythe Chorn and Peder Michael Pruzan-Jorgensen, "Supply Chain Sustainability: A Practical Guide for Continuous Improvement," UN Global Compact Office and Business for Social Responsibility (2010), https://www.bsr.org/reports/BSR_UNGC_SupplyChainReport.pdf (Accessed October 8, 2018).

10

Shaping Your Company Culture

The Team's Contribution to Culture
You have probably worked at a company that just didn't feel "right" or was not in alignment with your personality, values, or long-term goals. You might also have had the opportunity to work at companies that made you feel valued, appreciated, and part of a larger unit that promotes a greater good. Whether negative or positive, company culture is a large component of an employee's experience.

Every company has a unique culture that sets it apart from others. Company culture is difficult to quantify, but according to Investopedia, key aspects include: "dress code, business hours, office setup, employee benefits, turnover, hiring decisions, treatment of clients, client satisfaction and every other aspect of operations."[1] The way company management handles crises and conflicts, how they treat their employees, and overall office politics all factor in as well.

Many of the sustainability leaders interviewed shared that working on the Sustainability Team creates a sense of connection and cohesion other affinity groups lack. Since Sustainability Teams are most often composed of people from many different areas of the company (or even located throughout the world), they provide a unique opportunity for people to share ideas and resources, create solutions, and interact with co-workers they might never otherwise meet. At Salesforce, "There are 35+ groups around the world, so belonging to Earthforce gives employees a channel to collaborate with other employees who they would never meet or work with through their normal day jobs," says Ojure. "This enhances our culture of collaboration, innovation, fun, and giving back."

Sustainability Teams can make a significant contribution to a positive company culture by creating a shared vision and turning that passion into projects and campaigns that educate and improve life for the workforce and community.

Inspired Culture
Some Sustainability Teams may be simple, focused on reaching a few modest goals throughout the year. Others may be more complex, reaching into the entire business plan. In either case, employees contributing

to the Sustainability Team create meaningful change within the company and reduce its environmental footprint. When a company supports a Sustainability Team and integrates its initiatives into all aspects of the business (such as human resources, marketing, and operations), team members who are committed to bridging the gap between business and the environment feel more dedicated and loyal to their work.

The employees serving on the Dr. Bronner's Green Team go above and beyond their day-to-day responsibilities by working on sustainability issues. Their investment helps create a sense of connection and cohesion among everyone in the company. Participating in the Green Team builds a "sense of family" in a group of people from all different departments. It is a culture of closeness that is unique to this activist soap company.

The family-feeling company culture at Dr. Bronner's, and especially among those on the blossoming Green Team, significantly contributes to the high standards of quality reflected in their products (boosting their profits by extension!). In addition to pleasing customers, this culture attracts high-quality workers. Josh Alvarado, from the company's Shipping Department, elaborates:

> "Before I started working here, I was going through an existential crisis. I saw the company's philosophy it was promoting and tried very hard to get a job here. You don't have to necessarily believe in a religion or anything like that, but if you understand that we're

on this earth together, floating through space, we need to take care of each other. And we take care of each other in the company. It all makes perfect sense."

Shiber-Knowles shares, "first and foremost we are a business and profit is the engine that makes all of our impact possible." However, as she sees it, the Dr. Bronner's culture of excellence contributes to their business success as well as team dynamics. One example is that until a few years ago, there was no formal quality management system in place. The process was already first-nature to their committed workforce. Team members naturally took it upon themselves to investigate and analyze the quality of products. Shiber-Knowles believes this attention to detail is a result of the investment the owners make in employees through wages and benefits and the healthy relationships among employees who are personally invested in the company and are proud of the products it produces. "Invest in your people and allow relationships to grow and you will see those investments pay off in the product and in the bottom line," she insists.

Green Wisdom on a Global Scale
Your Sustainability Teams can create a sense of unity, whether your company has one office or many around the world. Even if events and campaigns differ from place to place, participating in the collective work of the Sustainability Team promotes a sense of alignment and connection among people in different cities.

With offices all over the globe, Earthforce volunteers bring Salesforce's awareness of environmental and social issues to bear on each geographic location. Despite the distance that separates them, there is a strong bond between the Earthforce members in each office. Each Earthforce team shares information about their efforts in their community with teams in other offices in other cities so that everyone has awareness about sustainability issues throughout the world. "One of the beautiful things about having these 7,000+ folks around the world is that they are our local champions. So they might be from any area of the business, in any role, but they typically work on a range of issues," explains Ojure.

With the help of the Earthforce members in San Francisco, Ojure and team create templates and tools, providing the structure that global Earthforce volunteers use to execute campaigns and events, as well as supporting satellite teams to plan communications that will help their efforts be more successful.

Quarterly global themes encourage volunteers to create initiatives concurrently, while still maintaining their individual flavor. Themes focus on issues such as energy, water, sustainable food, sustainable fashion, waste, and more, depending on what is important in the local region. Team members enjoy this "freedom within a framework." It fosters individuality while also uniting diverse offices in the advancement of Earthforce's overall mission. While Ojure's team oversees the creation of the monthly themes, "It's really up to the team leaders and the local offices to choose what really excites them and go with what they're passionate regarding the specifics about how a campaign will be executed.

Within this framework, Earthforce team members might be on the ground volunteering with local, environmentally-focused nonprofits, or they might emphasize employee engagement programs, such as inviting speakers to share their wisdom on plastic pollution prevention or water reduction. "My perception is that they really appreciate this balance of being able to take ownership and run with ideas that they're passionate about, [and] have a connection to headquarters while also feeling a sense of connection to the other Earthforce teams," Ojure shares. "We're all in this together!"

Though larger programs vary, Earthforce volunteers in all offices also focus on classic green team activities, such as creating messaging to remind everyone to conserve energy or recycle in the breakroom.

Sustainability Retains Talent
Businesses with Sustainability Teams are attractive to intelligent, innovative, values-driven people who want to make a difference. A 2016 study conducted by Cone Communications showed that 75% of Millennials take a company's social and environmental initiatives into consideration when choosing an employer, and the same number of people would take a pay cut to work at a company with responsible values.[2] When job-seekers choose between a company that has comprehensive, well-regarded, and effective sustainability initiatives and a company that doesn't, most will choose the former.

When employees have a stake in company policies, and especially company sustainability initiatives, they are more dedicated to all parts of the operation. That dedication reduces employee turnover, which in turn, reduces the expensive costs of recruiting and training. Retaining top talent—especially those who have a passion for sustainability—encourages future leaders, who possess invaluable business knowledge, to continue contributing to the company's success.

HR departments have not missed this trend and now recognize that sustainability programs can be used to recruit, retain, and inspire the workforce. Until you fully engage employees in your sustainability initiatives, you are ignoring one of your most dynamic and powerful tools for building a culture of commitment and a competitive edge.

Company Culture as an Energizing Force
Sustainability Teams motivate team members to work together to reach common goals and cultivate relationships that might not usually occur. The "Dr. Bronner's treat-each-other-like-family" ethos strengthens collaboration, trust, and communication. Shiber-Knowles believes that these characteristics drive business initiatives forward because people feel protected. "When you pay attention to relationships, everything gets easier," she shares.

The power of cultivating common goals is illustrated by the Dr. Bronner's "All-One" declaration, which sets a clear path forward for their sustainability efforts. Since Dr. Bronner's supports a wide range of social issues, the desire to decrease cost must be filtered through a higher imperative. "Our mission as a company is to create environmentally sustainable and socially just products of the highest quality and to use our profits to fund and fight for the causes we believe in," Shiber-Knowles explains. "Anything that we do to reduce the impact of our products in their creation or lifecycle that will save the company money will help us to meet our mission."

Even if a Sustainability Team does not have a direct influence on the product or service (as in the case of New Resource Bank, where the Green Team does not choose the companies to whom the bank lends), the fact that it exists adds to a company's culture, which contributes to employee commitment, loyalty, and dedication to the business. A company's culture can be the reason people love to come to work and stay for many years.

At Better World Books, "Those serving on the [Sustainability] Council are passionate about BWB's mission, passionate about sustainability, and are driven to make a difference in the world," shares Holland. "They share that enthusiasm with their co-workers and evangelize the company's mission at every opportunity. Our employees are mission-aligned," he continues, "and stick with the company through the good times and the bad times."

Dr. Bronner's sees the Sustainability Team as a chance to show their employees how much they are valued. As Shiber-Knowles shares, "the ideas of a junior level warehouse employee and a senior level corporate employee are considered equally on the team. Those interactions strengthen our "All-One" mission as well as our company bottom line, and I think will infuse the company culture in positive ways we cannot yet predict."

An Environmental Stewardship orientation session is part of each new employee's education at Self-Help Credit Union and Ventures Fund. Sessions are held quarterly via video conference so that new employees get to know each other while they are learning about the organization's culture of sustainability. After attending an orientation, staff receive a follow-up survey offering several options for staying involved in environmental stewardship, such as joining the email distribution list, "adopting" a compost bin or becoming a team ambassador. Knowing which aspects of sustainability are important to new employees helps to further shape Self-Help's culture.

"I think it's very helpful for individual staff members to be able to bring their environmental values to work—even if their job description is not directly related to environmental protection," says Malkin-Weber. "Our environmental stewardship umbrella gives a point of connection for someone who works in, for example, database administration, to be empowered to come up with good ideas for greening the organization, and also to feel connected to the sustainability work happening on other teams." This is yet another example of a cross-functional contribution that is a huge benefit not only to the employee but to the entire company.

Culture Catalysts
Your company culture can either inspire and energize or deflate and discourage. For people who are passionate about living in a world with clean air and water and eager to contribute to a positive future, working at a company that does not acknowledge climate change is difficult, if not impossible. But even employees who aren't personally committed to

environmental causes benefit from the energy and ethos that a well-functioning Sustainability Team brings to a business. A group of committed team members who rely on creativity and collaboration to solve problems and build community can only be an asset to your corporate culture.

Gratitude Puts Everything into Perspective

Team members are continually pulled in different directions due to the many responsibilities each juggles while balancing their paid positions with their passion projects. Reigniting the momentum after a setback through appreciation and gratitude can be the best way to get the team back on track.

Despite Dr. Bronner's not reaching their waste reduction goals in 2017 (for 2016 waste), Shiber-Knowles understands that keeping everything in perspective and being persistent will pay off for the team in the future. She shared that not improving their waste reduction goals was a step back, but bringing gratitude into their conversations supports how they work together going forward.

"There was a Dean that I worked with when I was in school who started every meeting with gratitude," she recalls. "He would thank the students at the beginning of the meeting in a genuine and applicable way, and I found that it really set the right tone, as it brought people into the room in a different way. It wasn't contrived and it wasn't forced. It was leadership offering genuine gratitude for the work being done, and people were then more present."

Shiber-Knowles took this approach to heart and now aims to start every meeting or conversation with a gratitude practice. Even if the topic of conversation is good news, she sees this as a way to create a connection between herself and members of the team.

> *"We're lucky to be here and we're lucky to work for a company that is an engine for positive change. There's plenty of inspiration to go around. If we pause and look, we'll see that there's plenty of good work happening, and be reminded that this is who we are as a company and as a community and as a family. If we say thank you for the things that others have done so far, then if there's bad news, such as the fact that we didn't reach our waste goals and there was cardboard that went to landfill, then it doesn't come across as demoralizing. It comes across as an opportunity for conversation about who we are, who we want to be and how do we get better. [Our] gratitude practices help us move past all of that so we continue to learn. We can draw strength for the future from the identity of the company, which is the tone that the Bronner family has set all along."*

Notes

1. "Corporate Culture," Investopedia (2018), https://www.investopedia.com/terms/c/corporate-culture.asp (Accessed October 8, 2018).
2. "2016 Cone Communications Millennial Employee Engagement Study," Cone Communications (April, 2016), p. 6, https://static1.squarespace.com/static/56b4a7472b8dde3df5b7013f/t/5819e8b303596e3016ca0d9c/1478092981243/2016+Cone+Communications+Millennial+Employee+Engagement+Study_Press+Release+and+Fact+Sheet.pdf (Accessed October 8, 2018).

11

The Power of Proof

Reporting Your Team's Accomplishments
You've created your Sustainability Team. You've set some goals and developed initiatives that are engaging, educational, and embrace a sense of community so that everyone involved is inspired and ready to take action.

Some of the programs your team created may have focused on employee education, with the hope that employees will transfer their new green wisdom to their homes and integrate it into their daily lives. Other company initiatives may have focused on community outreach, such as partnering with a local non-profit to plant succulents in a place where water-consuming grass once grew. And like many Sustainability Teams, you have probably also devised initiatives to decrease waste, energy, and other resources aggressively.

What does a Sustainability Team do with all of the information it gathers along the way?

Report it!

Reporting these changes to a local, regional, national, or international standards board and certification organization will help your company calibrate current benchmarks and support you in achieving your goals and improving future performance. Sharing your company's sustainability progress in this manner is an effective way to create clear communication and strengthen trust between the company and all stakeholders, such as employees, community members, vendors, investors, and shareholders. Reporting to a reputable standards board also demonstrates that your company is serious about sustainability and its effects on the planet.

There are many reporting and certification organizations. Some are organized and led by your local government, and others are tools used by large and small companies all over the world. The trick is to determine which reporting standard or certification organization is the best fit for your company. The following pages offer information about a few different types of frameworks that can be used to guide your Sustainability Team's initiatives and programs. While this is not a comprehensive list, it will keep you, your Sustainability Team, and your company moving in the right direction.

"Proving" that your Sustainability Team's efforts have been valuable, impactful, and a good return on the time and financial investment is an incredible milestone to meet!

Good luck, and please share your Sustainability Team's progress with me at nikki@alegriapartners.com.

Comprehensive Resources

The following organizations provide some of the most widely-used reporting tools and frameworks, useful across a broad spectrum of industries:

B Corp

A certified B Corp is a for-profit corporation that has been assessed by B Lab, a non-profit company that uses the B Impact Assessment to measure a company's social and environmental performance, public transparency, and legal accountability against their rigorous certification standards. Companies pursue this voluntary, third-party verification, along with many others, to promote positive change in the business world.

Being a member of the B Corp community is valuable for businesses because it provides a set of external standards that help your company demonstrate that your stakeholders are as (if not more) important as your shareholders. Also, in a world in which some 90-

plus percent of environmental product claims are guilty of greenwashing,[1] the New York Times explains, "B Corp provides what is lacking elsewhere: proof."[2]

For more information on B Corporation membership, please see the "pullout" section in Chapter One. B Corp members featured in this book include Better World Books, Badger Balm, Dr. Bronner's, Alter Eco, New Resource Bank, and Nutiva.
www.bcorporation.net

Fair Trade
Fair Trade began in the 1960s to help those struggling with poverty gain access to major markets. Decades later, the movement has many nodes and networks, all focused on a market-based approach to alleviating poverty and promoting environmentally sustainable development. For the consumer, this is seen most clearly through the certification and endorsement of individual products with the Fair Trade stamp.

Important to note is that the United States has two unique organizations certifying Fair Trade products. Fair Trade USA and Fair Trade America. Both groups were born out of Fairtrade International, but in 2011 Fair Trade USA left their parent organization, in the words of President and CEO Paul Rice, "in order to eliminate [certification] inconsistencies which exclude so many from the benefits of Fair Trade."[3] Fair Trade America began in 2013 as the new Fair Trade International organization.

Both organizations require adherence to standards of production, workforce equity, and environmental impact, and in exchange provide businesses or products with an internationally recognized seal of approval and market base. They differ mostly in governance and who they include in the certification, with Fair Trade USA pursuing a "higher-volume approach" including larger farms and plantations.

Certification allows recognized companies to market under an internationally recognized umbrella and access a large global market. A 2017 Globescan study of US consumers found that 81% would view an already-purchased brand more favorably if it carried the FairTrade Mark.[4] Fairtrade International's annual report also notes a 5% rise in the sale of Fairtrade-certified products in 2016 to a market of nearly $1.07 billion.[5]

Fair Trade USA offers product certification for coffee, produce & floral, seafood, apparel, and home goods, and consumer packaged goods, a spread that closely mirrors Fair Trade America.

Both organizations provide third-party certifications to rigorous standards and requirements that can be used to guide overall corporate sustainability practices and metrics.
www.fairtradeamerica.org
www.fairtradecertified.org

Global Reporting Initiative (GRI)
GRI is an independent international organization that has been on the front lines of sustainability reporting since 1997. Their Sustainability Reporting Standards are available at no cost as a "free public good." Approximately two-thirds of the world's 250 largest companies use GRI standards to report on their sustainability practices.

One of the many services GRI provides to help companies and organizations understand and report their impact on crucial sustainability initiatives is a "Reporting Starter Kit." The kit helps organizations of all kinds develop sustainability reports in line with GRI standards. The "GRI Support Suite" is a resource cycle that is designed to mirror the steps of the reporting process and provide all the necessary tools and services needed for developing each stage of the report.

As GRI describes, "By using the GRI Guidelines, reporting organizations disclose their most critical impacts – be they positive or negative – on the environment, society and the economy. They can generate reliable, relevant and standardized information with which to assess opportunities and risks, and enable more informed decision-making – both within the business and among its stakeholders. G4 is designed to be universally applicable to all organizations of all types and sectors, large and small, across the world."

In addition to maintaining the standard system, GRI offers a variety of services to help with preparation, alignment, communication, and analysis.

Alaska Airlines prepared their 2016 Sustainability Report in accordance with GRI's G4 Sustainability Reporting Guidelines Core option. In addition to using GRI's framework for reporting, they sought the help of third-party experts for the emissions and GHG portions of their review. Salesforce also created their 2017 Stakeholder Impact Report following the GRI standards.
www.globalreporting.org

*Please note that the G4 Guidelines have since been superseded by the GRI Standards.

Greenhouse Gas Protocol

Greenhouse Gas Protocol is the product of "a 20-year partnership between World Resources Institute (WRI) and the World Business Council for Sustainable Development (WBCSD)." The Protocol, which is the most widely used greenhouse gas accounting standard in the world (they claim that "in 2016, 92% of Fortune 500 companies responding to the CDP used GHG Protocol directly or indirectly through a program based on GHG Protocol."[6]) is designed to work for a wide range of reporters, from national governments to individual organizations.

Essentially GHG Protocol provides a standardized framework for tracking and reporting GHG emissions on a corporate level, including value-chain impact. The organization offers tools, trainings, an accounting platform, and a widely-used review service.

Genentech's 2016 Sustainability Data and Trends Report was produced in line with WRI GHG Protocol Scope 2 guidance. Salesforce also quantifies their Scope 1, 2, and 3 GHG emissions according to GHG Protocol definitions.
www.ghgprotocol.org

ISO 26000

The International Organization for Standardization has published over 22,000 international standards. Some of the most familiar guides are ISO 9000, ISO 14000, and ISO 26000.

In short, ISO 9000 is a set of standards for quality management systems, ISO 14000 covers environmental management systems, and ISO 26000 guides social responsibility. Each standard is nothing more and nothing less than a document explaining and standardizing best practices and practical information to help create globally compatible solutions to significant problems. A major goal of all ISO guidelines is to bring the all-too-often hidden costs of business into the open and quantify their impact, so they can become universally considered and understood factors in business decisions.

Though most organizations producing sustainability standards also offer certifications in those standards, ISO does not. They produce the standardized guidelines but do not themselves offer certifications. That said, a wide variety of external certification bodies do, and standards like ISO 9000 were designed with third-party certification in mind.

However, this is not true for ISO 26000! Launched in 2010, the goal of ISO 26000 is to define what social responsibility is, help "businesses and organizations translate principles into effective actions," and share "best practices relating to social responsibility, globally. It is aimed at all types of organizations regardless of their activity, size or location."

ISO 26000 is not a management system and does not outline requirements which can be certified. Its stated goal is to "assist organizations in contributing to sustainable development" by unpacking seven core subjects of social responsibility. The instruction provided supports many of the best practices described in this book and is an invaluable tool for understanding what social responsibility looks like in the sphere of business.

A library of resources is available to help translate that guidance into practical steps towards the UN Global Compact SDGs, for example, which can be reported on and verified.
www.iso.org

Sustainability Accounting Standards Board (SASB)
SASB is a private organization that develops and maintains sustainability accounting standards. Their standards cover 79 industries, providing a wide range of research and reporting resources.

Through an 18-month process, SASB researches which sustainability issues have the most bottom-line impact for your specific industry and then provides you with an industry-tailored standard, outlining how to disclose the most relevant information to your investors and stakeholders.

Their research platform, Navigator, helps you visualize and understand the sustainability-related risks and opportunities that are most pertinent to your operations, provides benchmarks for your sustainability goals, and allows you to focus on the elements of sustainability that generate the most value for your company.
www.sasb.org

TRUE Zero Waste Certification Program/US Zero Waste Business Council
The TRUE Zero Waste certification is a systems-based approach that focuses on lifecycle analysis of all

products used within a facility, helping businesses reuse all products and divert all solid waste from landfills, incinerators, and the environment, effectively eliminating waste.

Most important to note in regards to the Zero Waste certification is that the USZWBC has been integrated into Green Business Certification Inc. and in 2017 was rebranded as TRUE Zero Waste (apparently they realized USZWBC doesn't roll off the tongue).

Achieving TRUE Zero Waste certification provides a myriad of tangible benefits. Increased resource efficiency reduces costs and product reuse means waste streams become profit streams. Facilities operating in compliance with the certification standards manage risks, reduce GHG emissions, and invest resources locally.

The certification is available for any physical facility and the related operations. As of 2016, the Zero Waste certification was also ruled an acceptable stand-in for a variety of LEED Building Operation and Maintenance prerequisites and credits.

Certification is achieved by scoring at least 31 of 81 possible credit points on the TRUE Zero Waste scorecard and complying with seven essential program requirements. In addition to redesign and upstream management, points can also be scored through leadership, training, reporting, and innovation.

Nutiva, featured in the chapter four pullout, achieved a Gold Standard Zero Waste certification from USZWBC. Mountain Rose Herbs was the first Zero

Waste Certified company in the state of Oregon, receiving the highest designation, Platinum, for their efforts.
True.gbci.org

UN Global Compact (UNGC)
The United Nations Global Compact is an international organization created in 2000 to "mobilize a global movement of sustainable companies and stakeholders to create the world we want." The UNGC calls companies of all sizes and industries to align their actions with ten universal principles of sustainability and human rights.

Part of this goal is providing direction for the future. In 2015, leaders of 193 countries adopted 17 Sustainable Development Goals, or SDGs, as part of the 2030 Agenda for Sustainable Development at a UN Summit. Until recently, however, there was no structure in place to report on SDG progress.

That is no longer the case. UNGC has partnered with Global Reporting Initiative (GRI) and Principles for Responsible Investment (PRI) to develop a platform of resources to help companies report on SDG progress.

The 2018 platform involves four online learning labs that allow participants to interact with one another while learning how to report SDG progress and provide insight for the development of future tools and guidance.

To borrow language from UNGC's website, "Reporting on the SDGs aims to leverage the GRI Standards — the world's most widely used sustainability reporting standards — and the Ten Principles of the UN Global Compact. By doing so, businesses can incorporate SDG reporting into their existing processes, ultimately empowering them to act and make achieving the SDGs a reality."

Salesforce's 2018 Stakeholder Impact Report highlights their use of GRI metrics to support and report their progress towards the SDGs.
www.unglobalcompact.org

Zero Waste International Alliance
ZWIA was established to promote alternatives to landfills and incinerators, inspiring communities to stop thinking of waste as a problem and begin thinking about it as a resource that can fuel new products and jobs. They publish internationally recognized, peer-reviewed definitions and standards of Zero Waste.

One of Salesforce's public-facing goals is to "achieve zero-waste data centers in accordance with the Zero Waste International Alliance (90% landfill diversion from all data center sites)."[7]
www.zwia.org

Convergent Resources

These organizations provide more specialized tools and frameworks, tailored for use by specific industries:

Climate Collaborative
The Climate Collaborative is a non-profit created to catalyze bold action for climate change in the natural products industry. The organization brings manufacturers, retailers, brokers, distributors, and suppliers together to build existing climate solutions to scale and to find innovative, new ways to help reverse climate change.

Alter Eco, Badger Balm, Dr. Bronner's, Mountain Rose Herbs, and Nutiva have all made commitments to participate in the Climate Collaborative.
www.climatecollaborative.com

The Cool Farm Tool
In addition to a variety of research and resources, the Cool Farm Tool is an online calculator that helps growers measure greenhouse gases, water usage, and biodiversity. Becoming an alliance member supports the development of sustainable agriculture metrics and full access to the tool.
www.coolfarmtool.org

GMO Free
Currently, a claim to be "GMO-free" cannot be legally or scientifically backed due to the lack of definitive testing and the potential for all crops or products to be crossed or contaminated. Instead of indefensibly marketing as "GMO-free," groups like the Non-GMO Project offer standards and verification services which can be scientifically verified.

Non-GMO Project, the most widely recognized certification in the US, seeks to "preserve and build sources of non-GMO products, educate consumers, and provide verified non-GMO choices." Companies that are third-party verified as compliant with the Non-GMO Project Standard may display the Non-GMO Project Verified seal, which is the "fastest growing label in the natural products industry, representing $22.3 billion in annual sales and more than 50,000 verified products for over 3,000 brands."[8]

The verification process typically takes 3-6 months, depending on the type and number of products submitted. Non-GMO Project uses four third-party technical administrators to complete the verification process, which each have unique services and prices.

Dr. Bronner's products are Non-GMO Project Verified, in addition to a selection of Mountain Rose Herbs products.
www.nongmoproject.org

Leadership in Energy & Environmental Design (LEED)
The US Green Building Council's LEED rating system has become the most widely used green building standard in the world. The triple-bottom-line focus of LEED certification verifies best practices in "design, construction, operations, and maintenance of resource-efficient, high-performing, healthy, cost-effective buildings."

To achieve certification, building projects pursue credits that earn points towards the LEED rating system that best fits their project.
leed.usgbc.org

Leaping Bunny
The Leaping Bunny Standard (also known as the Corporate Standard of Compassion for Animals), is a voluntary supply-chain pledge to remove animal testing from all stages of development and production within cosmetic, personal care, and household products. The Leaping Bunny Program offers a cost-free annual product certification that has become an internationally recognized standard.
www.leapingbunny.org

Fair for Life
The complementary For Life and Fair for Life Standards cover "respect for human rights and fair working conditions. Respect of the ecosystem and promotion of biodiversity, sustainable agriculture practices" and "respect and betterment of local impact."

Fair For Life is a product-specific certification that verifies fair trade compliant supply chains. For Life is a company-wide CSR certification program. These third-party certifications are based upon International Fair Trade definitions and ISO 26000 guidelines among others.

Certification can be pursued for food products, cosmetic and beauty products, textiles, artisanal products, and natural ingredient products. Organic certified agricultural practices are encouraged but not required.

Dr. Bronner's main ingredients are fair trade certified through the Fair for Life Social and Fair Trade Certification and "was the first company to establish certified fair trade supply chains for coconut oil and palm oil." Mountain Rose Herbs has been a Fair for Life Certified company since 2010.
http://www.fairforlife.org/

Global Alliance for Banking on Values
GABV is a global network of leaders in the banking industry. They strive to lead the banking industry towards increased transparency and social, economic, and environmental sustainability through collaboration and education. Members must meet six criteria of leadership, values, and structure, and in return gain access to support and resources in advocating for values-based banking.
www.gabv.org

Green Business Network at Green America
Since 1982, the Green Business Network at Green America has evaluated over 8,000 businesses using 42 industry standards for green business. The breadth of their industry-specific assessments and the accessibility of their online certification process, which is geared towards small business owners, makes their Green Business Certification a remarkably attainable goal for even small-scale operations.

Certification includes access to listings in the National Green Pages and Green America's consumer base of 200,000. In partnership with B-Lab, Green America's Green Business Certification can be used to file for

Benefit Corporation status, one of the few eligible third-party standards.

Membership, which starts at only $130, includes access to the certification platform, ensuring that your pursuit of sustainability recognition (and the right to display that Green America Seal) won't break your bank.

Self-Help Credit Union, Dr. Bronner's, and Nutiva are all members of the Green Business Network.
www.greenbusinessnetwork.org

NATRUE
Responding to the difficulties of navigating complex international regulations and the lack of clear regulatory definitions for Natural and Organic Cosmetic products, NATRUE was launched in 2008. In the decade since release, nearly 6,000 products have been verified by NATRUE certification standards, providing consumers and manufacturers a clear way to distinguish their genuinely natural cosmetic products from greenwashing claims.
www.natrue.org

USDA NOP Organic
The National Organic Program provides oversight and regulation for nation-wide standards for organic agricultural produce as well as accreditation of certifying agents. They also maintain the National List of Allowed and Prohibited Substances for organic agriculture. As of 2015, organic products represent $43 billion of US retail sales.[9]
ams.usda.gov/NOP

NSF/ANSI 305 Cosmetic Organic

NOP organic requirements are typically geared toward produce, which can rule out many cosmetic and personal care products due to the chemical and production methods required in the cosmetics industry. However, if at least 70% of the product ingredients are certified organic, the product can be certified as NSF/ANSI 305 compliant. The Organic Trade Association recognizes this certification as best practice, and certified products may bear the NSF "contains organic ingredients label."
www.nsf.org

Vegan Action

Vegan Action provides individualized product certification for packaged vegan products. The annual fee is a sliding-scale based on the annual revenue of the certified product. Once certified, the product may display the Certified Vegan Logo and Vegan Action will support marketing and advertising.
www.vegan.org

The Vegan Society

It seems fitting that the organization that created the word vegan in 1944 can also certify your vegan product. The Vegan Society registers individual products annually according to their Vegan Trademark standards. Once a product passes registration criteria, it may display the Vegan Trademark. The Vegan Society also promotes registered products and offers discounts on advertising and marketing services.
www.vegansociety.com

World Fair Trade Organization
WFTO is the largest global network of Fair Trade Organizations. They use the WFTO Guarantee System to verify member compliance with the "10 Principles of Fair Trade" and continually maintain the WFTO Fair Trade Standard. Though the Guarantee System is not a product certification, it provides accountability and development support for fair trade supply chains, and members that pass the Guarantee System may use the WFTO label on products and are recognized as a "Guaranteed Fair Trade Organisation."
www.wfto.com

Corporate Commitment

The following is a membership organization for both individuals and businesses that require a declared commitment to climate change goals:

We Are Still In
We Are Still In is a network of over 2,700 leaders in business, government, universities, and non-profits committed to helping the U.S. meet its emissions reduction goals under the Paris Agreement. Actions include committing to powering operations with 100 percent renewable energy and harnessing collective purchasing power to hasten the adoption of renewable energy across the U.S. Many innovative climate change organizations, such as such as the B Team, The American Sustainable Business Council and the Environmental Defense Fund (to name a few), support this organization.

Alter Eco, Dr. Bronner's, Interface, Nutiva, and Salesforce have all made climate change commitments in alignment with We Are Still In. www.wearestillin.org

Notes

1. Richard Dahl, "Green Washing: Do You Know What You're Buying?" *Environmental Health Perspectives* 118(6) (2010), A246-A252, https://www.ncbi.nlm.nih.gov/pmc/articles/PMC2898878/ (Accessed October 8, 2018).

2. Tina Rosenberg, "Ethical Businesses With a Better Bottom Line," The New York Times (April 14, 2011), https://opinionator.blogs.nytimes.com/2011/04/14/ethical-businesses-with-a-better-bottom-line/ (Accessed October 8, 2018).

3. Paul Rice, "Fair Trade USA: Why We Parted Ways with Fair Trade International," Triple Pundit (January 11, 2012), https://www.triplepundit.com/2012/01/fair-trade-all-fair-trade-usa-plans-double-impact-2015/ (Accessed October 8, 2018).

4. "Certify Your Products," Fairtrade America (2018) http://fairtradeamerica.org/For-Business/Ways-of-Working-with-Fairtrade (Accessed October 8, 2018).

5. Ben Cooper, "Why There is Room for Two US fair Trade Organisations in US," Just-Food.com (December 20, 2017), https://www.just-food.com/analysis/why-

there-is-room-for-two-us-fair-trade-organisations-in-us_id138393.aspx (Accessed October 8, 2018).

6. "Standards," Greenhouse Gas Protocol (2018) https://ghgprotocol.org/standards (Accessed October 8, 2018).

7. "Global Environmental Policy," Salesforce (2018), https://www.salesforce.com/content/dam/web/en_us/www/assets/pdf/datasheets/sfdc-global-environmental-policy-2018.pdf (Accessed October 8, 2018).

8. "Verification FAQs," Non-GMO Project (2018) https://www.nongmoproject.org/product-verification/verification-faqs/ (Accessed October 8, 2018).

9. "Benefits of Organic Certification," United States Department of Agriculture (2018), https://www.ams.usda.gov/services/organic-certification/benefits (Accessed October 8, 2018).

My heartfelt thanks and love goes out to all the humans who helped me make this book happen at different steps of the way.

Thank you to those who freely shared their Green Wisdom:

Jay Coen Gilbert	B Corporation
Mike McGrory	B Corporation
Jess Baum	Badger
Rebecca Hamilton	Badger
Dustin Holland	Better World Books
Darcy Shiber-Knowles	Dr. Bronner's
Katie Excoffier	Genentech
Fran Teplitz	Green America
Mikhail Davis	Interface
Tony Cooper	Market Force
Alyssa Lawless	Mountain Rose Herb Company
Sunya Ojure	Salesforce
Melissa Malkin-Weber	Self Help Credit Union
Jacqueline Drumheller	formerly with Alaska Airlines
Gretchen Grani	formerly with Nutiva
Stephanie Meade	formerly with New Resource Bank

Thank you to those who supported me to make the meetings happen:

Callie Rojewski	B Lab
Clint Wilder	Clean Edge Consulting
Chris Allieri	Companies v. Climate Change
Jason Youner	Companies v. Climate Change
Jeff Marcous	Dharma Merchant Services
Tracy Tinclair	New Resource Bank
Kari Dorth	Presidio Graduate School
Pam Gordon	Presidio Graduate School

Thank you to those who worked alongside me, edited my words, or shared thoughts and energy to help make Green Wisdom come to fruition:

Cindy Belz
George Cisneros
Rose Diamond
Maura Fallon-McKnight
Silvan Fey
Ellen Goldberg
Suzette Hibble
Megan Hunt
Joel Johnson
George Kao
Ben Lizardi
Lorenzo Lizardi
James Lizardi
Jess Robertson
Jason Schneider
Tauni Swenson
Laura Wald
and all my friends from focusmate.com

Made in the
USA
Middletown, DE